Tipping recommendations

Hotel bills are all-inclusive. Though restaurant bills feature a 10 per cent service charge, it is usual to tip the waiter 5 to 10 per cent.

The sums we suggest are given in US dollars rather than dinar as the latter are subject to rapid inflation. Calculate your tip on the current dollar exchange rate. The amounts below represent normal tips for average middle-grade establishments.

Barber/Hairdresser	10%
Lavatory attendant	$ 0.25
Maid, per week	$ 3
Porter, per bag	$ 0.50
Taxi driver	optional
Tour guide	5–10%
Bus driver on excursions	$ 0.50

BERLITZ PHRASE BOOKS

World's bestselling phrase books feature not only expressions and vocabulary you'll need, but also travel tips, useful facts and pronunciation throughout. The handiest and most readable conversation aid available.

Arabic	French	Polish
Chinese	German	Portuguese
Danish	Greek	Russian
Dutch	Hebrew	Serbo-Croatian
European (14 languages)	Hungarian	Spanish
	Italian	Lat.-Am. Spanish
European Menu Reader	Japanese	Swahili
	Korean	Swedish
Finnish	Norwegian	Turkish

BERLITZ CASSETTEPAKS

The above-mentioned titles are also available combined with a cassette to help you improve your accent. A helpful miniscript is included containing the complete text of the dual language hi-fi recording.

BERLITZ®

SERBO-CROATIAN

FOR TRAVELLERS

By the staff of Berlitz Guides

Preface

You are about to visit Yugoslavia. Our aim is to give you a new and more practical type of phrase book to help you on your trip.

Serbo-Croatian for Travellers provides:

* all the phrases and supplementary vocabulary you will need on your trip

* a wide variety of tourist and travel facts, tips and useful information

* a complete phonetic transcription, showing you the pronunciation of all the words and phrases listed

* special sections showing the replies your listener might give to you – just hand him the book and let him point to the appropriate phrase. This is especially practical in certain difficult situations (doctor, car mechanic, etc.). It makes direct, quick and sure communication possible

* a logical system of presentation so that you can find the right phrase for the immediate situation

* quick reference through colour coding. The major features of the contents are on the back cover; a complete index is given inside.

These are just a few of the practical advantages. In addition, the book will prove a valuable introduction to life in Yugoslavia.

There is a comprehensive section on Eating Out, giving translations and explanations for practically anything one would find on a menu in Yugoslavia; there is a complete Shopping

6

Guide that will enable you to obtain virtually anything you want. Trouble with the car? Turn to the mechanic's manual with its dual-language instructions. Feeling ill? Our medical section provides the most rapid communication possible between you and the doctor.

To make the most of *Serbo-Croatian for Travellers,* we suggest that you start with the "Guide to Pronunciation". Then go on to "Some Basic Expressions". This not only gives you a minimum vocabulary; it helps you to pronounce the language.

We are particularly grateful to Dr. Naum R. Dimitrijević and to Mr. Rudolf Farkaš for their help in the preparation of this book, and also to Dr.T.J.A. Bennett for his help in creating the phonetic transcription. Additionally, we wish to thank the Yugoslav National Tourist Office for its assistance.

We shall be very pleased to receive any comments, criticisms and suggestions that you think may help us in preparing future editions.

Thank you. Have a good trip.

Guide to pronunciation

The alphabet

Two different alphabets are used in Yugoslavia. Our Roman alphabet is in use in Slovenia and Croatia; elsewhere the Cyrillic alphabet (more or less like the Russian one) is dominant. Given below are the characters which the Cyrillic alphabet, as used in Yugoslavia, comprises. The column at left shows the printed capital and small letters while written letters are shown in the center column. At right the corresponding letters are shown in the Roman alphabet which we're using in this book.

Printed	Written	Roman
А а		a
Б б		b
Ц ц		c
Ч ч		č
Ћ ћ		ć
Д д		d
Џ џ		dž (cap. **Dž**)
Ђ ђ		dj or đ (cap. **Dj** or **Đ**)
Е е		e
Ф ф		f
Г г		g
Х х		h
И и		i
Ј ј		j
К к		k
Л л		l
Љ љ		lj (cap. **Lj**)
М м		m
Н н		n
Њ њ		nj (cap. **Nj**)
О о		o
П п		p
Р р		r
С с		s
Ш ш		š
Т т		t
У у		u
В в		v
З з		z
Ж ж		ž

This, of course, is not enough to pronounce Serbo-Croatian. We're offering you a helping hand by providing "imitated pronunciation" throughout this book. This and the following chapter are intended to make you familiar with the transcription we devised and to help you get used to the sounds of Serbo-Croatian.

As a minimum vocabulary for your trip, we have selected a number of basic words and phrases under the title "Some Basic Expressions" (pages 11–16).

An outline of the sounds of Serbo-Croatian

You will find the pronunciation of the Serbo-Croatian letters and sounds explained below, as well as the symbols we're using for them in the transcriptions. Note that Serbo-Croatian has some diacritical letters – with accent marks – which we do not know in English. On the other hand, **q, w, x** and **y** do not exist in Serbo-Croatian. A basic rule for handling Serbo-Croatian might be: pronounce it as it's written – every letter is pronounced, and its pronunciation is always the same, regardless of its position in a word.

The imitated pronunciation should be read as if it were English, bearing in mind that there are no "silent" letters in our transcriptions except for any special rules set out below. Of course, the sounds of any two languages are never exactly the same; but if you follow carefully the indications supplied here, you will have no difficulty in reading our transcriptions in such a way as to make yourself understood. After that, listening to the native speakers on the record and constant practice will help you to improve your accent.

In the transcriptions, letters shown in bold print should be read with more stress (louder) than the others.

Consonants

Letter	Approximate pronunciation	Symbol	Example	
b	like b in brother	b	**brat**	braht
c	like ts in tse-tse	ts	**cesta**	tsehstah
č	like ch in church	ch	**čuti**	chootee
ć	like ch in cheap (a little further forward in the mouth than č; called a "soft" č)	ch	**ćerka**	chehrkah
d	like d in down	d	**dole**	doleh
dž	like j in June	j	**džem**	jehm
dj	like j in jeep (a "soft" dž); also written đ	j	**djak**	jahk
f	like f in father	f	**figura**	feegoorah
g	like g in go	g	**gde**	gdeh
h	like h in house	h	**hleb**	hlehb
j	like y in yoke	y	**ja**	yah
k	like k in key	k	**kuća**	koochah
l	like l in lip	l	**lep**	lehp
lj	like l in failure	lʸ	**ljubav**	lʸoobahv
m	like m in mouth	m	**most**	most
n	like n in not	n	**ne**	neh
nj	like ni in onion	ñ	**njegov**	ñehgov
p	like p in put	p	**policija**	poleetseeyah
r	like r in rope	r	**reka**	rehkah
s	like s in sister	s	**sestra**	sehstrah
š	like sh in ship	sh	**šta**	shtah
t	like t in top	t	**tamo**	tahmo
v	like v in very	v	**vrlo**	verlo
z	like z in zip	z	**zvezda**	zvehzdah
ž	like s in pleasure	zh	**želim**	zhehleem

Note: The letter **r** can also act as a vowel, as for example, in the word **vrlo** or in the name of the island **Krk**; in this case, it should be pronounced rather like a Scottish r, e.g., **Krk** is pronounced kerk.

Vowels

a	like **a** in father	ah	**sat**	saht
e	like **e** in get	eh	**svet**	sveht
i	like **i** in it	ee	**iz**	eez
o	like **o** in hot	o	**ovde**	ovdeh
u	like **oo** in boom	oo	**put**	poot

Some basic expressions

Yes.	**Da.**	dah
No.	**Ne.**	neh
Please.	**Molim.**	moleem
Thank you.	**Hvala.**	hvahlah
Thank you very much.	**Hvala Vam mnogo.**	hvahlah vahm mnogo
That's all right.	**Molim.**	moleem

Greetings

Good morning.	**Dobro jutro.**	dobro yootro
Good afternoon.	**Dobar dan.**	dobahr dahn
Good evening.	**Dobro veče.**	dobro vehcheh
Good night.	**Laku noć.**	lahkoo noch
Good-bye.	**Zbogom.**	zbogom
See you later.	**Dovidjenja.**	doveejehnyah
This is Mr....	**Ovo je Gospodin...**	ovo yeh gospodeen
This is Mrs....	**Ovo je Gospodja...**	ovo yeh gospojah
This is Miss...	**Ovo je Gospodjica...**	ovo yeh gospojeetsa
I'm very pleased to meet you.	**Milo mi je da sam Vas upoznao.**	meelo mee yeh dah sahm vahs oopoznaho
How are you?	**Kako ste?**	kahko steh
Very well, thank you.	**Hvala, vrlo dobro.**	fahlah verlo dobro
And you?	**A Vi?**	ah vee
Fine.	**Dobro.**	dobro
Excuse me.	**Izvinite.**	eezveehneehteh

> There's often a difference in grammatical form depending upon whether the person speaking is a man or a woman. We've used masculine forms throughout in this book except in cases where the feminine seemed more appropriate.

Questions

Where?	**Gde?**	gdeh
Where is...?	**Gde je...?**	gdeh yeh
Where are...?	**Gde su...?**	gdeh soo
When?	**Kad?**	kahd
What?	**Šta?**	shtah
How?	**Kako?**	kahko
How much?	**Koliko?**	koleeko
How many?	**Koliko?**	koleeko
Who?	**Ko?..**	ko
Why?	**Zašto?**	zahshto
Which?	**Koji/Koja/Koje?**	koyee/koyah/koyeh
What do you call this?	**Kako se ovo zove?**	kahko seh ovo zoveh
What do you call that?	**Kako se zove ono?**	kahko seh zoveh ono
What does this mean?	**Šta ovo znači?**	shtah ovo znahchee
What does that mean?	**Šta ono znači?**	shtah ono znahchee

Do you speak...?

Do you speak English?	**Govorite li engleski?**	govoreeteh lee ehnglehskee
Do you speak German?	**Govorite li nemački?**	govoreeteh lee nehmahchkee
Do you speak French?	**Govorite li francuski?**	govoreeteh lee frahntsooskee
Do you speak Spanish?	**Govorite li španski?**	govoreeteh lee shpahnskee
Do you speak Italian?	**Govorite li italijanski?**	govoreeteh lee eetahleeyahnskee
Could you speak more slowly, please?	**Možete li govoriti sporije molim Vas?**	mozhehteh lee govoreetee sporeeyeh moleem vahs

Please point to the phrase in the book.	Pokažite mi molim Vas tu frazu u knjizi.	pokahzheeteh mee moleem vahs too frahzoo oo kňeezee
Just a minute. I'll see if I can find it in this book.	Samo trenutak. Videću da li mogu da je nadjem u knjizi.	sahmo trehnootahk. veedehchoo dah lee mogoo dah yeh nahjhem oo kňeezee
I understand.	Razumem.	rahzoomehm
I don't understand.	Ne razumem.	neh rahzoomehm

Can... ?

Can I have...?	Mogu li dobiti...?	mogoo lee dobeetee
Can we have...?	Možemo li dobiti...?	mozhehmo lee dobeetee
Can you show me...?	Možete li mi pokazati...?	mozhehteh lee mee pokahzahtee
Can you tell me...?	Možete li mi reći...?	mozhehteh lee mee rehchee
Can you help me, please?	Možete li mi pomoći molim Vas?	mozhehteh lee mee pomochee moleem vahs

Wanting

I'd like......	Želeo bih...	zhehleho beeh
We'd like...	Želeli bismo...	zhehlehlee beesmo
Please give me...	Molim Vas dajte mi...	moleem vahs dahyteh mee
Give it to me, please.	Dajte mi to molim Vas.	dahyteh mee to moleem vahs
Please bring me...	Molim Vas donesite mi...	moleem vahs donehseeteh mee

Bring it to me, please.	Donesite mi to molim Vas.	donehseeteh mee to moleem vahs
I'm hungry.	Gladan sam.	glahdahn sahm
I'm thirsty.	Žedan sam.	zhehdahn sahm
I'm tired.	Umoran sam.	oomorahn sahm
I'm lost.	Zalutao sam.	zahlootaho sahm
It's important.	Važno je.	vahzhno yeh
It's urgent.	Hitno je.	heetno yeh
Hurry up!	Požurite!	pozhooreeteh

It is/There is...

It is/it's...	To je...	to yeh
Is it...?	Da li je to...?	dah lee yeh to
It isn't...	To nije...	to neeyeh
There is/There are...	Ima...	eemah
Is there/Are there...?	Ima li...?	eemah lee
There isn't/There aren't...	Nema...	nehmah
There isn't/There aren't any.	Nema.	nehmah

A few common words

big/small	veliko/malo	vehleeko/mahlo
quick/slow	brzo/sporo	berzo/sporo
early/late	rano/kasno	rahno/kahsno

SOME BASIC EXPRESSIONS

cheap / expensive	**jeftino / skupo**	yehfteeno / skoopo
near / far	**blizu / daleko**	bleezoo / dahlehko
hot / cold	**vruće / hladno**	vroocheh / hlahdno
full / empty	**puno / prazno**	poono / prahznoh
easy / difficult	**lako / teško**	lahko / tehshko
heavy / light	**teško / lako**	tehshko / lahko
open / shut	**otvoreno / zatvoreno**	otvorehno / zahtvorehno
right / wrong	**tačno / pogrešno**	tahchno / pogreshno
old / new	**staro / novo**	stahro / novo
old / young	**star / mlad**	stahr / mlahd
beautiful / ugly	**lepo / ružno**	lehpo / roozhno
good / bad	**dobro / loše**	dobro / losheh
better / worse	**bolje / lošije**	bol^yeh / losheeyeh

A few prepositions and some more useful words

at	**kod**	kod
on	**na**	nah
in	**u**	oo
to	**ka**	kah
from	**od**	od
inside	**unutra**	oonootrah
outside	**napolju**	nahpol^yoo
up	**gore**	goreh
down	**dole**	doleh
before	**pre**	preh
after	**posle**	posleh

with	**sa**	sah
without	**bez**	behz
through	**kroz**	kroz
towards	**prema**	**preh**mah
until	**do**	do
during	**za vreme**	zah **vreh**meh
and	**i**	ee
or	**ili**	**ee**lee
not	**ne**	neh
nothing	**ništa**	**neesh**tah
none	**ni jedan**	nee **yeh**dahn
very	**vrlo**	**ver**lo
also	**takodje**	**tah**kojeh
soon	**uskoro**	**oos**koro
perhaps	**možda**	**mozh**dah
here	**ovde**	**ov**deh
there	**tamo**	**tah**mo
now	**sada**	**sah**dah
then	**tada**	**tah**dah

A very basic grammar

The language

Here are a few practical linguistic hints for the English-speaking visitor to Yugoslavia.

As a matter of fact, three different languages are spoken in Yugoslavia: Serbo-Croatian, Slovenian and Macedonian. These three have equal political and social status but Serbo-Croatian is the most widely known and used. Slovenian is spoken only in Slovenia, Macedonian in Macedonia and Serbo-Croatian in the rest of the country; the latter is also well known to all educated Slovenes and Macedonians. As regards foreign languages, German is widely understood in Croatia and Slovenia, and Italian along the coast. So try your luck on those, too, if you like.

There are slight differences between the version of Serbo-Croatian used in Serbia and the one used in Croatia. Spelling and pronunciation are not quite the same. However, this will not cause great trouble to the tourist. More important are the differences in vocabulary. Here are some of the most current of them:

	in Serbia	in Croatia
air	vazduh	zrak
bread	hleb	kruh
cinema (movies)	bioskop	kino
floor (storey)	sprat	kat
road	put (drum)	cesta
spoon	kašika	žlica
theatre	pozorište	kazalište
train	voz	vlak
university	univerzitet	sveučilište
week	nedelja	tjedan

In this book, we have tried to allow for these divergencies. Sometimes you will find alternatives for words, given in brackets [ ] in the Serbo-Croatian text. If your listener cannot understand your first expression, try the alternative in brackets.

GRAMMAR

Nouns

One of the most striking differences between English and Serbo-Croatian is that there are no definite or indefinite articles to accompany the nouns. **Dečak** means "boy" and "a boy" as well as "the boy". Which of these is meant exactly is inferred from the context, or sometimes by the use of demonstrative pronouns ("this" or "that").

Every noun has its own gender. There are three genders in Serbo-Croatian: masculine, feminine and neuter. They can be roughly distinguished as follows:

1. Nouns of masculine gender end in a consonant in the singular and generally in **-i** in the plural, e.g.:

hotel	hotel	**avion**	aeroplane
hoteli	hotels	**avioni**	aeroplanes

2. Nouns of feminine gender mostly end in **-a** in the singular and in **-e** in the plural, e.g.:

obala	coast	**reka**	river
obale	coasts	**reke**	rivers

3. Neuter nouns mostly end in **-e** (sometimes in **-o**) in the singular, and in the plural mostly in **-a,** e.g.:

more	sea	**selo**	village
mora	seas	**sela**	villages

There is a rather complicated system for declining these nouns. For each gender, there are seven different cases in singular and plural. These cases are formed by endings which are added to the nouns. To give you an idea, here is the declension in the singular of the masculine noun **put** (road), the feminine **žena** (woman) and neuter **dete** (child).

1. Nominative (who?)	put	žena	dete
2. Genitive (whose?)	puta	žene	deteta
3. Dative (to whom?)	putu	ženi	detetu
4. Accusative (whom?- dir. obj.)	put	ženu	dete
5. Vocative (used in address)	pute	ženo	dete
6. Instrumental (with what?)	putom	ženom	detetom
7. Locative (where?)	putu	ženi	detetu

Adjectives

Adjectives generally precede the noun they accompany. They correspond with the noun in gender, number and case, e.g.:

širok put	wide road	**široka reka**	wide river
široki putevi	wide roads	**široke reke**	wide rivers

Several suffixes are used to construct the comparative and superlative forms of adjectives. The most common way is the following: to form the comparative, add **-iji** to the adjective (in the feminine **-ija,** in the neuter **-ije**), e.g.:

star	old	jeftin	cheap
stariji	older	jeftiniji	cheaper
(-ija, -ije)		(-ija, -ije)	

Od is the equivalent of "than" when comparing two objects.

Ova soba je jeftinija od Vaše.   This room is cheaper than yours.

The superlative is constructed by adding the prefix **naj-** to the comparative form, e.g.:

stariji	older	jeftiniji	cheaper
najstariji	oldest	najjeftiniji	cheapest

GRAMMAR

Here are some frequently used adjectives which are not quite regular in the way they form their comparatives:

		Comparative	Superlative
far	dalek	dalji	najdalji
fast	brz	brži	najbrži
good	dobar	bolji	najbolji
large (big)	velik	veći	najveći
long	dug	duži	najduži
small	malen	manji	najmanji

The table below shows the demonstrative adjectives of the three genders in the nominative case:

	Masculine	Feminine	Neuter
this	ovaj	ova	ovo
that	taj	ta	to
these	ovi	ove	ova
those	ti	te	ta

Personal pronouns

Here's another important difference from English: the personal pronoun indicating the subject of the verb is usually omitted. It's just not necessary, for the ending of the verb already indicates it sufficiently. Also note the use of the polite form in the second person, **Vi,** which corresponds to the German **Sie** or the French **vous.**

I	ja	we	mi
you	ti/Vi	you	vi/Vi
he, she, it	on, ona, ono	they	oni

GRAMMAR

Verbs

The verb system in Serbo-Croatian is too complex to be explained in a few lines. Here we only have room to give you a basic idea of what it's like. Easily enough, however, the infinitive of verbs either ends in **-ti** or **-ći.**

The present tense of the verb "to go" is as follows:

(ja) idem	I go	**(mi) idemo**	we go
(ti) ideš	you go	**(vi) idete**	you go
(on) ide	he goes	**(oni) idu**	they go

As there's no continuous tense in Serbo-Croatian, **ja idem** means both "I'm going" and "I go".

... and here's the conjugation, in the present tense, of two important auxiliaries, "to have" and "to be".

imati (to have)		**biti** (to be)	
imam	imamo	sam	smo
imaš	imate	si	ste
ima	imaju	je	su

In the compound tenses, the past participle agrees always with the gender and number of the subject of the verb. This occurs regularly in our book, e.g.:

I've asked...	**Ja sam poručio...**	I've asked...	**Ja sam poručila...**
(said by a man)		(said by a woman)	

The negative form of the verb is usually made by inserting the word **ne** ("not") before the verb:

Idem.	I go.	**Ne idem.**	I don't go.

The interrogative is usually formed by placing **li** after the verb in the affirmative form of the sentence:

Idemo u Dobrovnik.	We're going to Dubrovnik.
Idemo li u Dubrovnik?	Are we going to Dubrovnik?

Arrival

You've arrived. Whether you've come by ship or plane, you'll have to go through passport and customs formalities (for car/border control, see page 145).

There's certain to be someone around who speaks English. That's why we're making this a brief section. What you want is to be off to your hotel in the shortest possible time. Here are the stages for a speedy departure.

ARRIVAL

Passport control

Here's my passport.	**Ovo je moj pasoš.**	ovo yeh moy pahsosh
I'll be staying...	**Ja ostajem...**	yah ostahyehm
a few days	**par dana**	pahr dahna
a week	**nedelju dana**	nehdehlyoo dahnah
two weeks	**dve nedelje**	dveh nehdehlyeh
a month	**mesec dana**	mehsehts dahnah
I don't know yet.	**Još ne znam.**	yosh neh znahm
I'm here on holidays.	**Ja sam ovde na odmoru.**	yah sahm ovdeh nah odmoroo
I'm here on business.	**Ja sam ovde poslovno.**	yah sahm ovdeh poslovno
I'm just passing through.	**Samo sam na proputovanju.**	sahmo sahm nah propootovahñoo

If things become difficult:

| I'm sorry, I don't understand. Is there anyone here who speaks English? | **Izvinite, ne razumem. Da li ima neko ko govori engleski?** | eezveeneeteh neh rahzoomehm. dah lee eemah nehko ko govoree ehnglehskee |

Customs

The chart below shows what you can bring in duty free.*

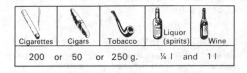

Cigarettes		Cigars		Tobacco		Liquor (spirits)		Wine
200	or	50	or	250 g.		¼ l	and	1 l

I've nothing to declare.	**Ja nemam ništa za carinjenje.**	ya **neh**mahm **nee**shtah zah tsahree**ñeh**ñeh
I've...	**Imam...**	ee**mahm**
a carton of cigarettes	**deset kutija cigareta**	**deh**seht **koo**teeyah tseegah-**reh**tah
a bottle of whisky	**jednu flašu viskija**	**yeh**dnoo **flah**shoo **vee**skeeyah
a bottle of wine	**jednu flašu vina**	**yeh**dnoo **flah**shoo **vee**nah
Must I pay on this?	**Moram li da platim za ovo?**	**mo**rahm lee dah **plah**teem zah **o**vo
How much?	**Koliko?**	**ko**leeko
It's for my personal use / it's not new.	**To je za moju ličnu upotrebu/to nije novo.**	to yeh zah **mo**yoo **leech**noo oopo**treh**boo/to **nee**yeh **no**vo

Possible answers

Morate platiti carinu za ovo.	You'll have to pay duty on this.
Platite, molim Vas, na šalteru preko.	Please pay at the office over there.
Imate li još prtljaga?	Have you any more luggage?
Otvorite, molim Vas, ovu torbu.	Open this bag, please.

---

* All allowances subject to change without notice.

ARRIVAL

Baggage – Porters

Porters in Yugoslavia won't take your bags through customs for you. You can give your bags to a porter only after you've passed through customs.

Porter!	**Nosač!**	nosach
What's your number?	**Koji je Vaš broj?**	koyee yeh vash broy
Can you help me with my luggage?	**Možete li mi poneti prtljag?**	mozhehteh lee me ponehtee pertl^yahg
That's mine.	**Ovo je moje.**	ovo yeh moyeh
That's my...	**To je moja...**	to yeh moyah
bag/luggage/suitcase	**torba/prtljag/kofer**	torbah/pertl^yahg/kofehr
That...one.	**Onaj...**	onahy
blue/brown/black big/small	**plavi/braon/crni veliki/mali**	plahvee/brahon/tsernee vehleekee/mahlee
There's one piece missing.	**Jedan komad nedostaje.**	yehdahn komahd nehdostahyeh
I'm looking for porter 19.	**Ja trižim nosača broj 19.**	yah trahzheem nosahchah broy 19
Take this bag to the...	**Odnesite ovu torbu do...**	odnehseeteh ovoo torboo do
taxi/bus/luggage lockers	**taksija/autobusa/ garderobe**	tahkseeyah/ahootoboosah/ gahrdehrobeh
Get me a taxi, please.	**Zovnite mi taksi, molim Vas.**	zovneeteh mee tahksee moleem vahs
Where's the bus for the railway station?	**Gde je autobus za železničku stanicu?**	gdeh yeh ahootoboos zah zhehlehzneechkoo stahneetsoo
How much is that?	**Koliko košta?**	koleeko koshtah

Note: There is no fixed charge for porters in Yugoslavia. The charge per bag depends on the distance it's carried and the city you're in.

Changing money

You'll find a banking service or a currency exchange office at most airports. If it's closed, don't worry. You'll be able to change money at your hotel.

Full details about money and exchange are given on pages 134-136.

Can you change a traveller's cheque (check)?	**Možete li mi promeniti putni ček?**	mozhehteh lee mee promehneetee pootnee chehk
I want to change some...	**Želim da promenim nekoliko...**	zhehleem dah promehneem nehkoleeko
traveller's cheques	**putnih čekova**	pootneeh chehkovah
dollars	**dolara**	dolahrah
pounds	**funti**	foontee
Where's the nearest currency exchange?	**Gde je najbliža menjačnica?**	gdeh yeh nahybleezhah mehñahchneetsah
What's the exchange rate?	**Kakav je kurs?**	kahkahv yeh koors

Directions

How do I get to...?	**Kako mogu doći do...?**	kahko mogoo dochee do
Is there a bus into town?	**Ima li autobus za grad?**	eemah lee ahootoboos zah grahd
Where can I get a taxi?	**Gde mogu naći taksi?**	gdeh mogoo nahchee tahksee
Where can I rent a car?	**Gde mogu da unajmim kola?**	gdeh mogoo dah oonahymeem kolah

Hotel reservations

Obviously, it's safer to book in advance if you can. But if you haven't done so?

Some terminals have a hotel reservation service and all have a tourist information office. There'll certainly be somebody there who speaks English.

FOR NUMBERS, see page 175

ARRIVAL

Car rental

Again, it's best to make arrangements in advance whenever possible. There are car rental firms at major airports and terminals, and in big cities and tourist places. It's very likely that someone there will speak English. But if nobody does, try one of the following...

I'd like...	**Želim...**	zhehleem
a car	**jedna kola**	yehdnah kolah
a small car	**mala kola**	mahlah kolah
a large car	**velika kola**	vehleekah kolah
a sportscar	**sportska kola**	sportskah kolah
I'd like it for...	**Trebaju mi za...**	trehbahyoo mee zah
a day	**jedan dan**	yehdahn dahn
four days	**četiri dana**	chehteeree dahnah
a week	**jednu nedelju**	yehdnoo nehdehl'oo
two weeks	**dve nedelje**	dveh nehdehl'eh
What's the charge per day?	**Koliko košta na dan?**	koleeko koshtah nah dahn
What's the charge per week?	**Koliko košta na nedelju?**	koleeko koshtah nah nehdehl'oo
Is that the low/high season rate?	**Da li je to cena van sezone/u sezoni?**	dah lee yeh to cehnah vahn sehzoneh/oo sehzonee
Does that include mileage?	**Da li to uključuje i kilometražu?**	dah lee to ookl'oocheeyeh ee keelomehtrahzhoo
Is petrol (gasoline) included?	**Da li je benzin uključen?**	dah lee yeh behnzeen ookl'oochehn
Does that include full insurance?	**Da li cena uključuje puno osiguranje?**	dah lee cehnah ookl'oo-chooyeh poono oseegoo-rahñeh
What's the deposit?	**Koliki je depozit [kaucija]?**	koleekee yeh dehpozeet [kahootseeyah]
I've a credit card.	**Ja imam kreditnu kartu.**	yah eemahm krehdeetnoo kahrtoo

FOR SIGHTSEEING, see page 75

Note: In Yugoslavia you may drive with your own licence; but check if an international permit is required for other countries you may visit.

Here's my driving licence.	**Izvolite moju vozačku dozvolu.**	eezvoleeteh moyoo vozahchkoo dozvoloo

Taxi

Cabs are available at ranks in all towns. City taxis have meters; in smaller towns, agree on a price in advance. Extra charges are levied for luggage and night travel. For some trips (e.g., airport to town) there may be a fixed rate. You can get the necessary information at the tourist information office.

Where can I get a taxi?	**Gde mogu da dobijem taksi?**	gdeh mogoo dah dobeeyehm tahksee
Get me a taxi, please.	**Zovnite mi, molim Vas, taksi.**	zovneeteh mee moleem vahs tahksee
What's the fare to...?	**Koliko košta do...?**	koleeko koshtah do
How far is it to...?	**Koliko ima do...?**	koleeko eemah do
Take me to...	**Odvezite me...**	odvehzeeteh meh
this address	**na ovu adresu**	nah ovoo ahdrehsoo
the town centre	**u centar grada**	oo tsehntahr grahdah
the...hotel	**u hotel...**	oo hotehl
Turn left (right) at the next corner.	**Skrenite levo (desno) na sledećem uglu.**	skrehneeteh lehvo (dehsno) nah slehdehchehm oogloo
Go straight ahead.	**Idite pravo.**	eedeeteh prahvo
Stop here, please.	**Stanite ovde, molim Vas.**	stahneeteh ovdeh moleem vahs
I'm in a hurry.	**Žurim se.**	zhooreem seh
There's no hurry.	**Bez žurbe.**	behz zhoorbeh
Could you drive more slowly?	**Vozite malo sporije, molim Vas.**	voozeeteh mahlo sporeeyeh moleem vahs

FOR TIPPING, see page 1

ARRIVAL

Hotel – Other accommodation

Early reservation (and confirmation) is essential in major tourist centres during the holiday season. Most towns have a tourist information office – and that's the place to go if you're stuck without a room.

Hotels in Yugoslavia are classified as follows:

Van kategorije (vahn kahtehgoreeyeh)	International luxury class; there are often only a few such hotels.
A-kategorija (ah-kahtehgoreeyah)	First-class, all facilities; suites, public rooms, conference rooms; some with indoor swimming pools, all bedrooms with private bath and toilet, telephone; some with TV
B-kategorija (beh-kahtehgoreeyah)	Comfortable; fairly good service, some bedrooms with private bath or shower, telephone
C-kategorija (tseh-kahtehgoreeyah)	Facilities and service limited; hotels of this category may vary according to the town
D-kategorija (deh-kahtehgoreeyah)	No running water; services very limited

In most hotels you can get *puni pansion* (**poo**nee pahn**see**on – full board) or *polupansion* (**po**loopahnseeon – bed and breakfast and one more meal, generally dinner).

Hotel prices are considerably reduced during off-season. Also, for long stays you can normally get a reduction on the daily rate.

A *pansion* (pahn**see**on – boarding house) sometimes has fewer facilities than a hotel. They're graded in three categories: I to III.

In popular resorts rooms (*soba* – **so**bah) in private homes often outnumber hotel rooms. They're closely supervised and graded (from I to IV), according to the degree of comfort provided and location.

HOTEL

In this section, we're mainly concerned with the smaller and middle-grade hotels. You'll have no language difficulties in the luxury and first-class hotels, where most of the staff have been trained to speak English.

In the next few pages we consider your requirements, step by step, from arrival to departure. You need not read through the whole lot; just turn to the situation that applies.

Reception – Checking in

My name is...	**Ja se zovem...**	yah seh zovehm
I've a reservation.	**Rezervisao sam.**	rehzehrveesaho sahm
We've reserved two rooms, a single and a double.	**Rezervisali smo dve sobe, jednu jedno-krevetnu i jednu dvokrevetnu sobu.**	rehzehrveesahlee smo dveh sobeh yehdnoo yehdno-krehvehtnoo ee yehdnoo dvokrehvehtnoo soboo
I wrote to you last month. Here's the confirmation.	**Pisao sam vam prošlog meseca. Izvolite potvrdu.**	peesaho sahm vahm proshlog mehsehtsah. eezvoleeteh potdverdoo
I'd like...	**Želeo bih...**	zhehleho beeh
a single room	**jednokrevetnu sobu**	yehdnokrehvehtnoo soboo
a double room	**dvokrevetnu sobu**	dvokrehvehtnoo soboo
two single rooms	**dve jednokrevetne sobe**	dveh yehdnokrehvehtneh sobeh
a room with twin beds	**sobu sa dva kreveta**	soboo sah dvah krehvehtah
with a bath	**sa kupatilom**	sah koopahteelom
with a shower	**sa tušem**	sah tooshehm
with a balcony	**sa balkonom**	sah bahlkonom
with a view	**sa pogledom**	sah poglehdom
a suite	**apartman**	ahpahrtmahn
We'd like a room...	**Mi želimo sobu...**	mee zhehleemo soboo
in the front/at the back	**s pogledom na ulicu/dvorište**	s poglehdom nah ooleetsoo/dvoreeshteh
facing the sea	**okrenutu moru**	okrehnootoo moroo
facing the courtyard	**okrenutu dvorištu**	okrehnootoo dvoreeshtoo

HOTEL

It must be quiet.	**Mora biti mirna.**	morah beetee meernah
I'd rather have something higher up/ lower down.	**Radije bih nešto više/niže.**	rahdeeyeh beeh nehshto veesheh/neezheh
Is there...?	**Ima li...?**	eemah lee
air conditioning	**klima uredjaj** [erkondišn]	kleemah oorehjahy [ehrkondeeshn]
central heating	**centralno grejanje**	tsehntrahlno grehyahñeh
radio	**radio**	rahdeeo
laundry/room service	**pranje rublja/ servis u sobi**	prahñeh roobl'ah/ sehrvees oo sobee
telephone	**telefon**	tehlehfon
television	**televizor**	tehlehveezor
private toilet	**zasebni toalet**	zahsehbnee toahleht
hot water/ running water	**topla voda/tekuća voda**	toplah vodah/teekoochah vodah

How much?

What's the price...?	**Koliko košta...?**	koleeko koshtah
per night	**za jednu noć**	zah yehdnoo noch
per week	**za nedelju**	zah nehdehl'oo
for bed and breakfast	**prenoćište sa doručkom**	prehnocheeshteh sah doroochkom
without meals	**bez hrane**	behz hrahneh
for full board	**puni pansion**	poonee pahnseeon
Does that include...?	**Da li to uključuje...?**	dah lee to ookl'oochooyeh
breakfast	**doručak**	doroochahk
meals	**ostale obroke**	ostahleh obrokeh
service	**servis**	sehrvees
Is there any reduction for children?	**Imaju li deca popust?**	eemahyoo lee dehtsah popoost
Do you charge for the baby?	**Da li se naplaćuje i za bebu?**	dah lee seh nahplahchooyeh ee zah behboo
That's too expensive.	**To je preskupo.**	to yeh prehskoopo
Haven't you anything cheaper?	**Imate li nešto jeftinije?**	eemahteh lee nehshto yehfteeneeyeh

FOR NUMBERS, see page 175

How long?

We'll be staying...	**Ostaćemo...**	ostahchehmo
overnight only	**samo jednu noć**	sahmo yehdnoo noch
a few days	**nekoliko dana**	nehkoleeko dahnah
a week (at least)	**(najmanje) jednu nedelju**	(nahymahñeh) yehdnoo nehdehl'oo
I don't know yet.	**Još ne znam.**	yosh neh znahm

Decision

May I see the room?	**Mogu li da vidim sobu?**	mogoo lee dah **vee**deem **so**boo
No, I don't like it.	**Ne, ne dopada mi se.**	neh neh **do**pahdah mee seh
It's too...	**Suviše je...**	**soo**veesheh yeh
cold/hot	**hladna/topla**	**hlah**dnah/**top**lah
dark/small	**mračna/malena**	**mrah**chnah/**mah**lehnah
noisy	**bučna**	**boo**chnah
No, that won't do at all.	**Ne, to uopšte ne odgovara.**	neh to **ooo**pshteh neh **od**govahrah
I asked for a room with a bath.	**Tražio sam sobu sa kupatilom.**	**trah**zheeo sahm **so**boo sah **koo**pahteelom
Have you anything...?	**Imate li nešto...?**	**ee**mahteh lee **neh**shto
better	**bolje**	**bol**'eh
bigger	**veće**	**veh**cheh
cheaper	**jeftinije**	**yehf**teeneeyeh
smaller	**manje**	**mah**ñeh
That's fine. I'll take it.	**Dobra je, uzeću je.**	**do**brah yeh **oo**zehchoo yeh

HOTEL

Bills

These are usually submitted weekly or when you leave if you stay less than a week. Some hotels offer a reduction for infants and children under 12.

FOR DAYS OF THE WEEK, see page 180

Tipping

The service charge (10%) is normally included in the bill. It might be just as well, however, to ask if service is included: *Da li je servis uključen?* (dah lee yeh **sehr**vees oo**klyoo**chehn). Tip the porter when he brings the bags to your room and tip the bellboy if he does any errands for you. So have small change ready.

Registration

Upon arrival in some hotels you'll be asked to fill out a registration form (*prijava* – **pree**yahvah). It requires details of your name, home address, passport and perhaps some other similar information It's almost certain to carry an English translation. If it doesn't, ask the desk clerk:

What does this mean? **Šta znači ovo?**   shtah **znah**chee ovo

The desk clerk will probably ask you for your passport. He may want to keep it for a while, even overnight. Don't worry. You'll get it back. He may want to ask you the following questions:

Mogu li videti Vaš pasoš?	May I see your passport?
Ispunite, molim Vas, ovaj formular.	Would you mind filling in this registration form?
Potpišite ovde, molim Vas.	Sign here, please.
Koliko dugo ostajete?	How long will you be staying?

Please have our bags sent up.	**Pošaljite molim Vas naš prtljag gore.**	poshahl'yeeteh moleem vahs nahsh pertl'rahg goreh
I'll take this briefcase with me.	**Ja ću poneti tašnu.**	yah choo ponehtee tahshnoo
What's my room number?	**Koji je broj moje sobe?**	koyee yeh broy moyeh sobeh

HOTEL

Service, please

Now that you're safely installed, meet some more of the hotel staff.

the bellboy	**dečko**	dehchko
the chambermaid	**sobarica**	sobahreetsah
the manager	**direktor**	deerehktor
the telephone operator	**telefonistkinja**	tehlehfoneestkeeñah
the valet	**sobar**	sobahr
the waiter	**kelner**	kehlnehr
the waitress	**kelnerica**	kehlnehreetsah

If you want to address members of the staff, don't say *gospodin* (gos**po**deen), *gospodja* (**go**spojah) or *gospodjica* (**go**spojeetsah), but use a general introductory phrase such as:

Excuse me. Could you..., please?	**Izvinite. Da li biste mogli molim Vas...**	eezvee**nee**teh. dah lee **bee**steh **mog**lee **mo**leem vahs

General requirements

Please ask the chambermaid to come up.	**Pošaljite molim Vas sobaricu.**	poshahlʸeeteh **mo**leem vahs sobahreetsoo
Who is it?	**Ko je?**	ko yeh
Just a minute?	**Samo trenutak.**	**sah**mo treh**noo**tahk
Come in!	**Slobodno!**	slobodno
Is there a bath on this floor?	**Ima li na ovom spratu kupatilo?**	**ee**mah lee nah ovom sprahtoo koopahteelo
How does this shower work?	**Kako radi ovaj tuš?**	**kah**ko **rah**dee ovahy toosh
Where's the plug for a shaver?	**Gde je utikač [štekdozna] za aparat za brijanje?**	gdeh yeh ooteekahch [shtehkdoznah] zah ahpahraht zah breeyahñeh
Please send up some coffee/sandwiches.	**Molim Vas pošaljite mi kafu/sendviče.**	**mo**leem vahs poshahlʸeeteh mee **kah**foo/**sehnd**veecheh
Can we have breakfast in our room?	**Možemo li dobiti doručak u sobi?**	**mo**zhehmo lee do**bee**tee do**roo**chahk oo **so**bee

I'd like to leave these in your safe.	Želim ovo da ostavim u vašem sefu.	zhehleem ovo dah ostahveem oo vahshehm sehfoo
Can you find me a baby-sitter for tonight?	Možete li mi naći nekog da čuva dete večeras?	mozhehteh lee mee nahchee nehkog dah choovah dehteh vehchehrahs
Can I have a/an/some...?	Mogu li da dobijem...	mogoo lee dah dobeeyehm
ashtray	pepeljaru	pehpehlʸahroo
bath towel	peškir za kupanje	pehshkeer zah koopahñeh
extra blanket	još jedno ćebe [deku]	yosh yehdno chehbeh [dehkoo]
envelopes	koverata	kovehrahtah
more hangers	još vešalica	yosh vehshahleetsah
hot-water bottle	termofor	tehrmofor
ice	leda	lehdah
needle and thread	iglu i konac	eegloo ee konahts
pillow	jastuk	yahstook
pillow case	jastučnicu	yahstoochneetsoo
reading lamp	lampu za čitanje	lahmpoo zah cheetahñeh
soap	sapun	sahpoon
writing paper	papira za pisanje	pahpeerah zah peesahñeh
Where's the...?	Gde je...?	gdeh yeh
beauty parlour	kozmetički salon	kozmehteechkee sahlon
cocktail lounge	snek bar	snehk bahr
dining room	sala za ručavanje	sahlah zah roochahvahñeh
hairdresser's	frizer	freezehr
restaurant	restoran	rehstorahn
television room	soba za televiziju	sobah zah tehlehveezeeyoo

Breakfast

The Yugoslavian breakfast generally consists of coffee (tea) and milk, rolls with butter and jam or honey. Some hotels, however, may serve an English breakfast.

Have you any...?	Imate li...?	eemahteh lee
eggs	jaja	yahyah
bacon and eggs	slaninu sa jajima	slahneenoo sah yahyeemah
boiled eggs	kuvana jaja	koovahnah yahyah
fried eggs	pržena jaja	perzhehnah yahyah
ham and eggs	šunku sa jajima	shoonkoo sah yahyeemah
scrambled eggs	kajganu	kahygahnoo

fruit juice	voćni sok	vochnee sok
grapefruit	grepfrut	grehpfroot
orange	pomorandža	pomorahnjah
pineapple	ananas	ahnahnahs
tomato	paradajz	pahrahdahyz
marmelade	marmaladu	mahrmahlahdoo
toast	prepržen hleb	prehperzhehn hlehb
May I have some...?	Mogu li dobiti...?	mogoo lee dobeetee
butter/chocolate	putera/čokolade	pootehrah/chokolahdeh
coffee/cream	kafu/slatke pavlake	kahfoo/skahtkeh pahvlahkeh
honey/lemon	med/limun	mehd/leemoon
milk/pepper	mleko/biber	mlehko/beebehr
salt/sugar	so/šećer	so/shehchehr
tea	čaj	chahy
Can you bring me a...?	Možete li mi doneti...?	mozhehteh lee mee donehtee
cup	šoljicu	shol'eetsoo
fork	viljušku	veel'ooshkoo
glass	čašu	chahshoo
knife	nož	nozh
plate	tanjir	tahñeer
spoon	kašiku	kahsheekoo

Note: You'll find a great many other dishes listed in our "Eating out" guide (pages 38-64). This should be consulted for your lunch and dinner menus.

Difficulties

The...doesn't work.	...ne radi.	...neh rahdee
air conditioner	klima uredjaj [erkondišn]	kleemah oorehjahy [ehrkondeeshn]
fan	ventilator	vehnteelahtor
faucet	slavina	slahveenah
heating	grejanje	grehyahñeh
light	svetlo	svehtlo
tap	pipa	peepah
toilet	toalet	toahleht
ventilator	ventilator	vehnteelahtor
The wash basin is blocked.	Lavabo je zapušen.	lahvahbo yeh zahpooshehn

HOTEL SERVICE

The window is jammed.	**Prozor ne može da se otvori.**	prozor neh mozheh dah seh otvoree
The blind is stuck.	**Zavesa ne može da se povuče.**	zahvehsah neh mozheh dah seh povoocheh
There's no hot water.	**Nema vruće vode.**	nehmah vroocheh vodeh
These aren't my shoes.	**Ovo nisu moje cipele.**	ovo neesoo moyeh tseepehleh
This isn't my laundry.	**Ovo nije moje rublje.**	ovo neeyeh moyeh roobl'eh
I've lost my watch/ key.	**Izgubio sam svoj sat/ključ.**	eezgoobeeo sahm svoy saht/kl'ooch
I've left my key in my room.	**Ostavio sam ključ u svojoj sobi.**	ostahveeo sahm kl'ooch oo moyoy sobee
The...is broken.	**...ne radi.**	...neh rahdee
bulb	**sijalica [žarulja]**	seeyahleetsah [zhahrool'ah]
lamp	**lampa**	lahmpah
plug	**utikač [šteker]**	ooteekahch [shtehkehr]
shutter	**roletne**	rolehtneh
switch	**prekidač [šalter]**	prehkeedahch [shahltehr]
window shade	**zavesa**	zahvehsah
Can you get it fixed?	**Možete li to popraviti?**	mozhehteh lee to poprahveetee

Telephone – Mail – Callers

Can you get me Vienna 12-34-56?	**Mogu li dobiti Beč, broj 12-34-56?**	mogoo lee dobeeteh behch broy 12-34-56
Did anyone ring for me?	**Da li me je neko nazvao?**	dah lee meh yeh nehko nahzvao
Operator, I've been cut off.	**Gospodjice, veza se prekinula.**	gospojeetseh vehzah seh prehkeenoolah
Is there any mail for me?	**Ima li pošte za mene?**	eemah lee poshteh zah mehneh
Have you any stamps?	**Imate li maraka?**	eemahteh lee mahrahkah
Would you post this for me, please?	**Hoćete li, molim Vas, ovo da predate na poštu?**	hochehteh lee moleem vahs ovo dah prehdahteh nah poshtoo
Are there any messages for me?	**Ima li kakvih poruka za mene?**	eemah lee kahkveeh porookah zah mehneh

FOR POST OFFICE, see page 137

Checking out

Can I have my bill, please?	Mogu li da dobijem račun, molim Vas?	mogoo lee dah dobeeyehm rahchoon moleem vahs
I'm leaving early tomorrow. Please have my bill ready.	Ja odlazim rano ujutro, molim Vas spremite moj račun.	yah odlahzeem rahno ooyootro moleem vahs sprehmeeteh moy rahchoon
We'll be checking out around noon.	Mi odlazimo oko podne.	mee odlahzeemo oko podneh
I've got to leave at once.	Moram da idem odmah.	morahm dah eedehm odmah
Does that include service?	Da li ovo uključuje i servis?	dah lee ovo ooklʲoochooyeh ee sehrvees
Is everything included?	Da li je sve uključeno?	dah lee yeh sveh ooklʲoochehno
You've made a mistake in this bill, I think.	Mislim da ste napravili grešku u računu.	meesleem dah steh nahprahveelee grehshkoo oo rahchoonoo
Can you get us a taxi?	Možete li nam pozvati taksi?	mozhehteh lee nahm pozvahteh tahksee
When's the next... to Belgrade?	Kad ima sledeći... za Beograd?	kahd eemah slehdehchee... zah behograhd
bus/train/plane	autobus/voz [vlak]/ avion	ahootoboos/voz [vlahk]/ ahveeon
Would you send someone to bring down our luggage?	Možete li poslati nekog da snese naš prtljag.	mozhehteh lee poslahteh nehkog dah snehseh nahsh pertlʲahg
We're in a great hurry.	Mi se jako žurimo.	mee seh yahko zhooreemo
Here's my forwarding address. You've got my home address.	Ovo je moja sledeća adresa. Vi imate moju kućnu adresu.	ovo yeh moyah slehdehchah ahdrehsah. vee eemahteh moyoo koochnoo ahdrehsoo
It's been a very enjoyable stay.	Ovde nam je bilo vrlo ugodno.	ovdeh nahm yeh beelo verlo oogodno
We hope to come again some day.	Nadamo se da ćemo opet doći.	nahdahmo seh dah chehmo opeht dochee

HOTEL SERVICE

FOR TAXI, see page 27

Eating out

There are several types of bars and restaurants in Yugoslavia. Some of them differ from each other only in name. Here are the main and most usual kinds of places you're likely to encounter.

Bar
(bahr)

A nightclub; generally with a floor show, sometimes with strip-tease; expensive

Bife
(beefeh)

Serves light meals or snacks, alcoholic and soft drinks; closes earlier than a *gostiona*

Dansing
(dahnseeng rehstorahn)

A café or restaurant where food is served together with drinks. Dance music is played

Ekspres restoran
(ehksprehs rehstorahn)

A self-service restaurant, cheaper than other restaurants; common in larger cities and seaside resorts; fairly limited selection of food and drinks

Gostiona
(gosteeonah)

An inn; serves meals and drinks

Kafana
(kahvahnah)

A café serving coffee, tea and alcoholic drinks, cakes and snacks

Krčma
(kerchmah)

is a synonym for *gostiona*. Mainly drinks, mediocre service

Mlečni restoran
(mlehchnee rehstorahn)

A "milk restaurant". Dairy products like milk, yogurt, rice pudding, etc., served, as well as light meals, cakes, pancakes and the like.

Pivnica
(peevneetsah)

A beer cellar; wine and other drinks are also available.

Restoran
(rehstorahn)

Yugoslavian restaurants, as all other, vary in cuisine and service. They're classified in the same way as hotels.

Riblji restoran
(reeblyee rehstorahn)

A restaurant serving mainly, but not exclusively, fish

Some restaurants display a menu in the window showing the table d'hôte meals with fixed prices, and the à la carte menu. Check if the service is included. Generally it is, but it does not harm to ask the waiter. Taxes aren't levied on restaurant meals.

Meal times

Breakfast (*doručak* – **do**roochahk) is served from 7 until 9 a.m.

Lunch (*ručak* – **roo**chahk) is the main meal in Yugoslavia; it's served from about noon until 2 or 3 p.m.

Dinner (*večera*–**veh**chehrah) is served from about 6.30 to 7 p.m. to 9.30 or 10 p.m. After this it's usually cold snacks only.

However, this timetable goes for hotel restaurants only. The *gostiona* (gostee**o**nah–inn) and other places of the kind serve meals almost the whole day until midnight and later.

What and where?

Yugoslavia is a great country for gastronomic explorers. The country's cuisine has been influenced by several cultures (Turkish, Greek, Austrian, Italian) and therefore offers a rich variety of styles of cooking and specialities within a relatively small range.

All along the coast, fish is the staple item on restaurant menus. The Dalmatian coast is also where you'll find the most Italian influence in cooking: dishes like pasta, *pršut* (**per**shoot – the Italian *prosciutto,* a kind of ham) and ravioli will remind you of the other side of the Adriatic. Strong Greek influence can be recognized in Macedonia (grilled meats); Bosnia-Herzegovina is rather Turkish-minded. And there's one trace of Turkey that you'll appreciate throughout the country: coffee. It's always good, thick and strong.

Wine (cheap!) and liquors are available in abundant variety. As concerns water: it may be better, especially in smaller places, to drink bottled water. Often the waiter will bring you a bottle of mineral water with your meal even without your asking for it. Yugoslavians like to mix it with their wine.

Hungry?

| I'm hungry/I'm thirsty. | Ja sam gladan/Ja sam žedan. | yah sahm **glah**dahn/yah sahm **zheh**dahn |
| Can you recommend a good (and inexpensive) restaurant? | Možete li preporučiti neki dobar (ne tako skup) restoran? | **mo**zhehteh lee prehporoo**chee**tee nehkee **do**bahr (neh **tah**ko skoop) reh**sto**rahn |

If you want to be sure of getting a table in well-known restaurants, it may be better to telephone in advance.

I'd like to reserve a table for four for eight o'clock tonight.	Želim da rezervišem jedan sto za četvoro za osam sati večeras.	zhehleem dah rehzehrvee-shehm yehdahn sto zah chehtvoro zah osahm sahtee vehchehrahs

Asking and ordering

Good evening, I'd like a table for three.	Dobro veče. Želeo bih sto za troje.	dobro vehcheh. zhehleho beeh sto zah troyeh
Could we have a...?	Možemo li dobiti...?	mozhehmo lee dobeetee
table in the corner	sto u uglu	sto oo oogloo
table by the window	sto pored prozora	sto porehd prozorah
table outside	sto napolju	sto nahpolʸoo
table on the terrace	sto na terasi	sto nah tehrahsee
quiet table somewhere	sto na mirnom mestu	sto nah meernom mehstoo
Where are the toilets?	Gde je toalet?	gdeh yeh toahleht
Can you serve me right away? I'm in a hurry.	Možete li me odmah poslužiti? Jako mi se žuri.	mozhehteh lee meh odmah posloozheeteh? yahko mee seh zhooree
What's the price of the fixed menu?	Koja je cena menia?	koyah yeh tsehnah mehneeah
Is service included?	Da li je servis uključen?	dah lee yeh sehrvees ooklʸoochehn
Could we have a(n)...please?	Možemo li, molim Vas, dobiti...	mozhehmo lee moleem vahs dobeetee
ashtray	pepeljaru	pehpehlʸahroo
bottle of...	flašu...	flahshoo
(another) chair	(još jednu) stolicu	(yosh yehdnoo) stoleetsoo
glass	čašu	chahsho˙
glass of water	čašu vode	chahshoo vodeh
knife	nož	nozh
napkin	salvetu	sahlʸvehtoo
plate	tanjir	tahñeer
spoon	kašiku	kahsheekoo
tablecloth	stolnjak	stolñahk
toothpick	čačkalicu	chahchkahleetsoo

EATING OUT

FOR COMPLAINTS, see page 55

EATING OUT

I'd like a/an/some…	Molim Vas…	moleem vahs
aperitif	**aperitiv**	ahpehreeteev
appetizer	**predjelo**	prehdyehlo
beer	**pivo**	peevo
bread	**kruh [hleb]**	krooh [hlehb]
butter	**puter**	pootehr
cabbage	**kupus**	koopoos
cheese	**sir**	seer
coffee	**kafu**	kahfoo
dessert	**dezert**	dehzehrt
fish	**ribu**	reeboo
french fries	**prženi krompir**	perzhehnee krompeer
fruit	**voće**	vocheh
game	**divljač**	deevlyahch
ice-cream	**sladoled**	slahdolehd
ketchup	**kečap**	kehchahp
lemon	**limun**	leemoon
lettuce	**salatu**	sahlahtoo
meat	**meso**	mehso
mineral water	**mineralnu vodu**	meenehrahlnoo vodoo
milk	**mleko**	mlehko
mustard	**senf**	sehnf
oil	**ulje**	oolyeh
olive oil	**maslinovo ulje**	mahsleenovo oolyeh
pepper	**biber**	beebehr
potatoes	**krompir**	krompeer
poultry	**živinsko meso**	zheeveensko mehso
rice	**pirinač**	peereenahch
rolls	**kajzericu**	kahyzehreetsoo
salad	**salatu**	sahlahtoo
salt	**so**	so
sandwich	**sendvič**	sehndveech
seasoning	**začin**	zahcheen
shellfish	**školjke**	shkolykeh
snack	**mezu**	mehzoo
soup	**supu**	soopoo
spaghetti	**špageti**	shpahgehtee
sugar	**šećer**	shehchehr
tea	**čaj**	chahy
vegetables	**povrće**	povercheh
vinegar	**sirće [ocat]**	seercheh [otsaht]
water	**vodu**	vodoo
wine	**vino**	veeno

What's on the menu?

Our menu has been arranged according to courses. Under each heading you'll find an alphabetical list of dishes in Serbo-Croatian with their English equivalents. These lists – which include everyday items and special dishes – will enable you to make the most of a Yugoslavian menu.

Here's our guide to good eating and drinking. Turn to the course you want.

	Page
Appetizers	44
Egg dishes	45
Soups	45
Fish and seafood	46
Meat	47
Fowl – Game	49
Vegetables and seasonings	49
Cheese	51
Fruit	52
Dessert	53
Alcoholic drinks	56
Other beverages	62
Eating light – Snacks	63

EATING OUT

Obviously, you're not going to go through every course. If you've had enough, say:

Nothing more, thanks.	**Ne hvala, bilo je dosta.**	neh **hvah**lah **bee**lo yeh **dos**tah

Appetizers – Starters

If you feel like something to whet your appetite, choose carefully, for Yugoslavian appetizers can be filling

I'd like an appetizer.	**Želeo bih neko predjelo.**	zhehleho beeh nehko prehdyehlo
What do you recommend?	**Šta mi preporučujete?**	shtah mee prehporoochooyehteh
burek s mesom	boorehk s mehsom	meat pasty
dagnji	dahgñee	mussels
dalmatinski sir	dahlmahteenskee seer	Dalmatian cheese
dimljeni losos	deemlyehnee losos	smoked salmon
domaća šunka	domahchah shoonkah	country ham
domaće kobasice	domahcheh kobahseetseh	home-made sausages
guščija džigerica	gooshcheeyah jeegehreetsah	goose liver
haringe	hahreengeh	herring
jastog	yahstog	lobster
kavijar	kahveeyahr	caviar
losos	losos	salmon
marinirana riba	mahreeneerahnah reebah	pickled fish
ostrige	ostreegeh	oysters
pašteta od džgirerice	pahshtehtah od jeegehreetseh	liver paste
pašteta od mesa	pahshtehtah od mehsah	meat paste
pršuta	pershootah	Dalmatian ham
punjene masline	pooñehneh mahsleeneh	stuffed olives
račići	rahcheechee	shrimp
riblji rižoto	reeblyee reezhoto	fish-rice casserole
ruska salata	rooskah sahlahtah	diced, cooked vegetables with mayonnaise
špargle	shpahrgleh	asparagus
šunka	shoonkah	ham
sušene haringe	sooshehneh hahreengeh	smoked herring
tunjevina	tooñehveenah	tunny (tuna)

Yugoslavian specialities

kajmak	kahymahk	a national speciality made from the skin of milk
praška šunka	prahshkah shoonkah	pressed ham
sremske kobasice	srehmskeh kobahseetseh	a very rich kind of sausage, made in Srem

Egg dishes

I'd like an omelet.	**Želeo bih jedan omlet od jaja.**	zhehleho beeh yehdahn omleht od yahyah
gibanica	geebahneetsah	a pasty with cheese and eggs
jaja u majonezu	yahyah oo mahyonehzoo	egg salad
omlet sa sirom	omleht sah seerom	cheese omelet
omlet sa šunkom	omleht sah shoonkom	ham omelet

Soups

A distinction has to be made between the clear soups, which are called *supa* (**soo**pah) or *juha* (**yoo**hah), and the thick soups, which are called *čorba* (**chor**bah).

I'd like some soup. What do you recommend?	**Želeo bih juhu. Šta mi preporučujete?**	zhehleho beeh yoohoo. shtah mee prehporoochooyehteh
alaška čorba	ahlahshkah chorbah	fish soup; also called *brodet*
boršč	borshch	borsch, a vegetable soup with various kinds of meat and cream
čorba od gljiva	chorbah od glʸeevah	mushroom soup
čorba od paradajza	chorbah od pahrahdahyzah	tomato soup
čorba od povrća	chorbah od poverchah	vegetable soup
govedja supa	govehjah soopah	beef soup
govedja supa sa jajem	govehjah soopah sah yahyehm	beef soup with an egg
jagnjeća čorba	yahgñehchah chorbah	lamb soup
konzome	konzomeh	consommé
pileća čorba	peelehchah chorbah	chicken soup with noodles
riblja čorba	reeblʸah chorbah	fish soup
teleća čorba s mesom	tehlehchah chorbah s mehsom	veal soup

EATING OUT

Fish and seafood

I want some fish.	**Željeo bih ribu.**	zhehleho beeh reeboo
What kinds of sea-food do you have?	**Koju vrstu ribe imate?**	koyoo verstoo reebeh eemahteh
bakalar	bahkahlahr	cod
barbun	bahrboon	red mullet
brancin	brahntseen	bass
cipoli	tseepolee	mullet
girice	geereetseh	pickerel
grgeč	gergehch	perch
haringa	hahreengah	herring
ikra	eekrah	roe
jastog	yahstog	lobster
jegulja	yehgool'yah	eel
jesetra	yehsehtrah	sturgeon
kamenice	kahmehneetseh	a kind of oyster
lignji	leegñee	squid
list	leest	plaice/sole
losos	losos	salmon
merlan	mehrlahn	whiting
mladica	mlahdeetsah	a kind of trout
mušule	mooshooleh	mussels
ostrige	ostreegeh	oysters
pastrmka	pahstermkah	trout
rakovi	rahkovee	crab
sanpiero	sahnpeeehro	John Dory
šaran	shahrahn	carp
sardela	sahrdehlah	anchovies
skampi	skahmpee	scampi
skuše	skoosheh	mackerel
som	som	catfish
srdele	serdehleh	pilchard
štuka	shtookah	pike
tunjevina	tooñehveenah	tunny (tuna)
zubatac	zoobahtahts	dentex

fried	**pržena**	perzhehnah
grilled	**na gradele (na roštilju)**	nah grahdehleh (nah roshteelyoo)
marinated	**marinirane**	mahreeneerahneh
poached	**kuvana (lešo)**	koovahnah (lehsho)
smoked	**dimljena**	deemlyehnah

Meat

I'd like some...	Željeo bih...	zhehleho beeh
beef	govedinu	govehdeenoo
pork	svinjetinu	sveeñehteenoo
veal	teletinu	tehlehteenoo
mutton	ovčetinu	ovchehteenoo

What kinds of meat have you got?	Koju vrstu mesa imate?	koyoo verstoo mehsah eemahteh
bubrezi	boobrehzee	kidneys
ćufte	choofteh	meatballs
džigerica	jeegehreetsah	liver
faširana govedina	fahsheerahnah govehdeenah	minced beef
govedina	govehdeenah	beef
govedje pečenje	govehjeh pehchehñeh	roast beef
jezik	yehzeek	tongue
jagnjeće grudi	yahgñehcheh groodee	breast of lamb
jagnjeći kotlet	yahgñehchee kotleht	lamb cutlet
jagnjetina	yahgñehteenah	lamb
junetina	yoonehteenah	young beef
kobasice	kobahseetseh	sausages
krezle	krehzleh	veal glands
kuvana šunka	koovahnah shoonkah	cooked ham
mozak	mozahk	brain
narezak	nahrehzahk	cold cuts
ovčetina	ovchehteenah	mutton
prasetina	prahsehteenah	suckling pig
pršuta	pershootah	Dalmatian ham
rebra	rehbrah	ribs
slanina	slahneenah	bacon
svinjska kolenica	sveenskah kolehneetsah	pig's knuckle
šnicl	shneetsl	veal scallop
šnicl bez kosti	shneetsl behz kostee	fillet
srce	sertseh	heart
šunka	shoonkah	ham
suva šunka	soovah shoonkah	cured ham
suva rebra	soovah rehbrah	smoked spare ribs
sveža šunka	svehzhah shoonkah	fresh ham
svinjetina	sveeñehteenah	pork
svinjska glava	sveeñskah glahvah	pig's head
svinjski kotlet	sveeñskee kotleht	pork chop
svinjsko pečenje	sveeñsko pehchehñeh	roast pork
teletina	tehlehteenah	veal

How do you like your meat?

boiled	**kuvano**	koovahno
braised	**dinstovano**	deenstovahno
fried	**prženo**	perzhehno
grilled	**na roštilju**	nah roshteel'oo
roast	**pečeno**	pehchehno
stewed	**kuvano u pari**	koovahno oo pahree
stuffed	**filovano**	feelovahno
rare	**nepečeno**	nehpehchehno
	[polupečeno]	[poloopehchehno]
medium	**srednje pečeno**	srehdñeh pehchehno
well done	**dobro pečeno**	dobro pehchehno

Some meat dishes

ćulbastija
(chool**bah**steeyah)
grilled veal or pork

ćevapčići
(chehvahpcheechee)
minced meat, grilled in rolled pieces

djuveč
(joovech)
casserole of lamb or pork with rice and green peppers

musaka
(moosahkah)
layers of minced meat and other, sliced potatoes or eggplant; egg and sour milk topping, oven-browned

pljeskavica
(plyehskahveetsah)
hamburger steak served with raw onion

punjene paprike
(poonyehneh pahpreekeh)
green peppers stuffed with minced meat and tomato sauce

ražnjići
(rahzhnyeechee)
small pieces of veal or pork, grilled on a skewer

sarma
(sahrmah)
cabbage leaves stuffed with minced meat and rice

vešalica
(vehshahleetsah)
grilled veal or pork (scrag)

EATING OUT

Fowl – Game

Hunting grounds still abound in Yugoslavia. Consequently, game is one dish you shouldn't miss if you're there during the season.

I'd like some game.	**Želeo bih divljač.**	zhehleho beeh **deev**lyahch
What poultry dishes do you serve?	**Kakvo živinsko meso imate?**	kahkvo zhee**veen**sko **meh**so ee**mah**teh
ćuretina	choorehteenah	turkey
divljač	deevlyahch	game
fazan	fahzahn	pheasant
golub	goloob	pigeon
jarebica	yahtehbeetsah	partridge
kunić	kooneech	rabbit
patka	pahtkah	duckling
pečena piletina	pehchehnah **pee**lehteenah	roast chicken
piletina	peelehteenah	chicken
prepelica	prehpehleetsah	quail
zečetina	zehchehteenah	hare
živina	zheeveenah	fowl

Vegetables and seasonings

What vegetables do you recommend?	**Koje povrće mi preporučujete?**	koyeh povercheh mee prehporoochooyehteh
I'd prefer some salad.	**Želeo bih salatu.**	zhehleho beeh sahlahtoo
artičoke	ahrteechokeh	artichoke
beli luk	behlee look	garlic
biber sa Jamajke	beebehr sah yahmaheekeh	pimiento
boranija	borahneeyah	haricot (french) beans
bundeva	boondehvah	pumpkin
celer	tsehlehr	celery
cvekla	tsvehklah	beetroot
gljive	glʸeeveh	mushrooms
gomoljica	gomolʸeetsah	truffles
grašak	grahshahk	peas
karfiol	kahrfeeol	cauliflower
kelj	kehlʸ	kale
kiseli kupus	keesehlee koopoos	sauerkraut
kozlac	kozlahts	tarragon
krastavac	krahstahvats	cucumber

EATING OUT

krastavci [kiseli]	krahstahvtsee [keesehlee]	gherkins, pickles
krstovnik	kerstovneek	watercress
krompir	krompeer	potatoes
kukuruz [kuvani ili pečeni]	kookoorooz [koovahnee eeleh pehchehnee]	corn on the cob
kupus	koopoos	cabbage
leće	lehcheh	lentils
luk	look	onions
majčina dušica	mahycheenah doosheetsah	thyme
mirodjija	meerojeeyah	caper
mirodjija u turšiji	meerojeeyah oo toorsheeyee	dill
mrkva	merkvah	carrot
paprike	pahpreekeh	green peppers
paradajz	pahrahdahyz	tomatoes
pasulj	pahsooly	beans
patlidžan	pahtleejahn	eggplant (aubergine)
peršun	pehrshoon	parsley
pirinač	peereenahch	rice
povrće	povehrcheh	vegetables
mešano povrće	mehshahno povercheh	mixed vegetables
praziluk	prahzeelook	leeks
prokula	prokoolah	brussels sprouts
ren	rehn	horseradish
repa	rehpah	beet
rotkvice	rotkveetseh	radishes
salata	sahlahtah	salad
sitni luk	seetnee look	chives
slatki biber	slahtkee beebehr	sweet pepper
spanać	spahnahch	spinach
špargle	shpahrgleh	asparagus
začini	zahcheenee	spices
zelena boranija	zehlehnah borahneeyah	green beans
zelena salata	zehlehnah sahlahtah	lettuce
zelje	zehlyeh	herbs
mešano zelje	mehshahno zehlyeh	mixed herbs
žutenica	zhootehneetsah	chicory

Vegetables may be served:

creamed	pasirano	pahseerahno
diced	seckano	sehtskahno
fried	prženo	perzhehno
grilled	grilovano	greelovahno
stewed	kuvano	koovahno

Cheese

There are many kinds of locally produced cheeses in Yugoslavia. If in a restaurant, ask the waiter. But you can also buy
them directly from farmers at the open-air markets.

Try some of these well-known Yugoslav cheeses:

belava (**beh**lahvah)	cottage cheese, mild and fat-free
kačkavalj (**kahch**kahvahlʲ)	rich cheese; may be mild or sharp, depending on its age
mladi srpski sir (**mlah**dee **serp**skee seer)	soft white cheese, with smooth texture; made from cow or sheep milk
paški sir (**pahsh**kee seer)	fat and fairly sharp cheese from the island of Pag
somborski sir (**som**borskee seer)	mild cheese made from cow milk, smooth texture
topfn (**topfn**)	the same as *belava*
trapist (**trah**peest)	there are several kinds of *trapist* cheeses, produced locally and varying from region to region
travnički sir (**trahv**neechkee seer)	rich and fairly salty cheese, made from sheep milk

In all better hotels, foreign-made cheeses are also available.
Kajmak (**kayh**mahk) is a rich and very tasty starter, made from
the skin of boiled milk. It can be eaten with bread or rolls.
Some dishes, for instance *ćevapčići* (cheh**vahp**cheechee – a local
speciality of minced and grilled meat), are sometimes prepared
with *kajmak* instead of oil or butter.

Fruit

Have you got fresh fruit?	Imate li svežeg voća?	eemahteh lee svehzhehg vochah
I'd like a fresh fruit salad.	Želeo bih voćnu salatu.	zhehleho beeh vochnoo sahlahtoo
ananas	ahnahnahs	pineapple
bademi	bahdehmee	almonds
banana	bahnahnah	banana
borovnica	borovneetsah	blueberries
breskve	brehskveh	peaches
brusnica	broosneetsah	cranberries
bundeva	boondehvah	pumpkin
dinja	deeñah	melon
dud	dood	mulberries
dunje	dooneh	quinces
grožđe	grozhjeh	grapes
jabuke	yahbookeh	apples
jagode	yahgodeh	strawberries
kajsije	kahyseeyeh	apricots
kesteni	kehstehneh	chestnuts
kokosov orah	kokosov orah	coconuts
kruške	krooshkeh	pears
kupine	koopeeneh	blackberries
lešnik	leshneek	hazelnuts
limun	leemoon	lemon
lubenica	loobehneetsah	watermelon
maline	mahleeneh	raspberries
mandarine	mahndahreeneh	tangerines
masline	mahsleeneh	olives
nar	nahr	pomegranate
ogrozl	ogrozl	gooseberries
orasi	orahsee	walnuts
pomorandža	pomorahnjah	orange
ribizla	reebeezlah	currants
ringlovi	reenglovee	greengage
šljive	shl'eeveh	plums
smokve	smokveh	figs
suve šljive	sooveh shl'eeveh	prunes
suvo grožđe	soovo grozhjeh	raisins
trešnje	trehshñeh	cherries
urme	oormeh	dates
višnje	veeshñeh	sour cherries

Dessert

If you have survived all the courses on the menu, you may want to order a dessert. Yugoslavian desserts may be fairly heavy, so be careful with your choice if you have a delicate digestion.

I'd like a dessert, please.	**Molim Vas dezert.**	moleem vahs dehzehrt
Nothing more, thanks.	**Ništa više, hvala lepo.**	neeshtah veesheh hvahlah lehpo
Something light, please.	**Nešto lagano, molim.**	nehshto lahgahno moleem
Just a small portion.	**Malu porciju, molim.**	mahloo portseeyoo moleem

If you are not sure what to order, ask the waiter:

What do you recommend?	**Šta preporučujete?**	shtah prehporoochooyehteh
baklava	bahklahvah	a Turkish pastry with syrup
kompot od jabuka	kompot od yahbookah	stewed apples
kompot od krušaka	kompot od krooshahkah	stewed pears
kompot mešani	kompot mehshahnee	stewed mixed fruit
palačinke	pahlahcheenkeh	pancakes
sa džemom	sah jehmom	with jam
sa orasima	sah orahseemah	with walnuts
sa prelivom od jaja	sah prehleevom od yahyah	with egg flip
sa sirom	sah seerom	with cheese
pešmelba	pehshmehlbah	peach melba
pita od jabuka	peetah od yahbookah	apple strudel
pita od sira	peetah od seerah	cheese strudel
sladoled	slahdolehd	ice cream
od čokolade	od chokolahdeh	chocolate
od jagoda	od yahgodah	strawberry
od limuna	od leemoonah	lemon
od vanilije	od vahneeleeyeh	vanilla
suva pita sa orasima	soovah peetah sah orahseemah	walnut cake
torta od čokolade	tortah od chokolahdeh	chocolate cake
torta od voća	tortah od vochah	fruit cake
bez šlaga	behz shlahgah	without whipped cream
sa šlagom	sah shlahgom	with whipped cream

EATING OUT

The bill (check)

May I have the bill (check), please?	**Račun, molim.**	rahchoon moleem
Haven't you made a mistake?	**Da niste pogrešili?**	dah neesteh pogrehsheelee
Is service included?	**Da li je servis uključen?**	dah lee yeh sehrvees ookloochehn
Is everything included?	**Da li je sve uključeno?**	dah lee yeh sveh ookloochehno
I haven't any small change.	**Nemam sitno.**	nehmahm seetno
Can I charge it on a credit card?	**Mogu li platiti kreditnom kartom?**	mogoo lee plahteetee krehdeetnom kahrtom
Do you accept traveller's cheques?	**Da li primate putne čekove?**	dah lee preemahteh pootneh chehkoveh
Thank you, this is for you.	**Hvala, to je za Vas.**	hvahlah to yeh zah vahs
Keep the change.	**Zadržite sitninu.**	zahderzheeteh seetneenoo
That was a very good meal. We enjoyed it, thank you.	**Vrlo dobro smo jeli. Bilo nam je vrlo prijatno, hvala Vam.**	verlo dobro smo yehlee. beelo nahm yeh verlo preeyahtno hvahlah vahm
We'll come again sometime.	**Doći ćemo opet.**	dochee chehmo opeht

```
SERVIS UKLJUČEN
SERVICE INCLUDED
```

EATING OUT

Complaints

But perhaps you'll have something to complain about...

There's a draught here. Could you give us another table?	**Ovde je promaja. Možete li nam dati drugi sto?**	ovdeh yeh promahyah mozhehteh lee nahm dahtee droogee sto
That's not what I ordered. I asked for...	**To nisam poručio, ja sam poručio (poručila*)...**	to neesahm poroocheeo yah sahm poroocheeo (poroocheelah)
I don't like this.	**Ovo mi se ne dopada.**	ovo mee seh neh dopahdah
I can't eat this.	**To ne mogu da jedem.**	to neh mogoo dah yehdehm
May I change this?	**Mogu li ovo da promenim?**	mogoo lee ovo dah promehneem
The meat is...	**Meso je...**	mehso yeh
overdone	**prepečeno**	prehpehchehno
underdone	**nedopečeno**	nehdopehchehno
too rare	**suviše sirovo**	sooveesheh seerovo
too tough	**suviše žilavo**	sooveesheh zheelahvo
This is too...	**Ovo je suviše...**	ovo yeh sooveesheh
sweet	**slatko**	slahtko
bitter	**gorko**	gorko
salty	**slano**	slahno
The food is cold.	**Hrana je hladna.**	hrahnah yeh hlahdnah
This is not fresh.	**Ovo nije sveže.**	ovo neeyeh svehzheh
There's a fly in my soup.	**Muva je u mojoj supi.**	moovah yeh oo moyoy soopee
Would you ask the head waiter to come over?	**Hoćete zamoliti glavnog kelnera da dodje?**	hochehteh lee zahmoleetee glahvnog kehlnehrah dah dojeh

EATING OUT

---

*Feminine. See Grammar.

Drinks

Beer

Beer is called *pivo* (**pee**vo) in Serbo-Croatian. In Yugoslavia, most large cities have their own brewery. Some are as many as 250 years old. The quality of the beer varies. Generally speaking, there are two kinds of beer: light (*svetlo* – **sveh**tlo) and dark (*crno* – **tser**no). Light beer is the one most commonly drunk in Yugoslavia. There is also *specijalno pivo* (speh**tsee**yahlno **pee**vo), extra strong beer compared with the other two. In some places, you'll find *dijetalno pivo* (deeyeh**tahl**no **pee**vo), a special beer for diabetics.

As a rule, beer is sold in bottles. There are relatively few places where draught (draft) beer is available. If you like cold beer, be sure to ask for it.

I'd like a bottle of beer.	**Želeo bih flašu piva.**	**zheh**leho beeh flahshoo **pee**vah
A cold beer, please.	**Hladno pivo, molim Vas.**	**hlahd**no **pee**vo moleem vahs

Wine

Wine is called *vino* (**vee**no) in Serbo-Croatian. If you are travelling through the country, try the local wines. This is not just a matter of economy; it may be your only chance to sample it, since many wines don't "travel" well. Some wines are available only in the area where they are produced.

Local wines are generally sold as table wine, not bottled. As a rule, table wine is cheaper and often of just as good quality as bottled wine. But sometimes you may be offered artificial (*veštačko* – **vehsh**tahchko) wine; therefore, ask:

Is this wine natural?	**Da li je vino prirodno?**	dah lee yeh **vee**no **pree**rodno

EATING OUT

Together with the wine, the waiter will most probably bring you a bottle of soda water. If he doesn't, say:

| A bottle of soda water, please. | **Flašu soda vode molim.** | fl**a**hshoo sodah vodeh moleem |

If you don't want him to pour some into your wine, tell him:

| Without soda water, please. | **Bez soda vode molim.** | behz sodah vodeh moleem |

Quite a few Yugoslavians are fond of *špricer* (**shpree**tsehr), wine mixed with soda water. In some areas, on the Dalmatian coast for example, people very often drink what is called *bevanda* (**beh**vahndah): wine and water.

The best known Yugoslavian wines come from Slovenia (*Slovenačka vina* – **slo**vehnahchka **vee**nah), Dalmatia (*Dalmatinska vina* – dahl**mah**teenskah **vee**nah) and from some parts of Serbia. The wines from Serbia as well as from certain other parts of the country are named after the region where they are produced: *Smederevka* (**smeh**dehrehvkah – wine from Smederevo, Serbia), *Fruškogorska vina* (**froo**shkogorskah **vee**nah – wines from Fruška Gora), etc.

If you want the wine list, ask the waiter: *Vinsku kartu molim* (**veen**sko **kahr**too **mo**leem).

Here are some of the better known wines:

Crno župsko (tsehrno zhoopsko)	a dry red wine
Dingač (deengahch)	red, full-bodied
Fruškogorski biser (frooshkogorskee beesehr)	a sparkling, champagne-like wine; medium dry
Graševina (grahshehveenah)	dry white
Jervin Muskat Hamburg (yehrveen mooskaht hahmboorg)	a sweet and heavy red wine

EATING OUT

Ljutomer
(lyootomehr)

a white wine, slightly sweet; this wine is very popular abroad

Mapa
(mahpah)

a dry rosé

Muškat otonel
(mooshkaht otonehl)

a light white wine, dry and flavoured

Pošip
(posheep)

Dalmatian, very dry

Prokupac
(prokoopahts)

a red wine, sweet and light

Prošek
(proshehk)

a famous sweet Dalmatian wine; the colour depends on the kind

Rizling
(reezleeng)

a dry, white wine (from different parts of the country)

Rubinova ružica
(roobeenovah roozheetsah)

dry rosé

Semijon
(sehmeeyohn)

very dry white

Traminac
(trahmeenahts)

a white wine; drier than *Muškat*

Vršačko belo
(vehrshahchko behlo)

a light white wine

Žilavka
(zheelahvkah)

a dry white wine from Herzegovina

I'd like...of...	**Želeo bih...**	zhehleho beeh...
a bottle	**flašu**	flahshoo
half a bottle	**pola flaše**	polah flahsheh
a glass	**čašu**	chahshoo
a litre	**litru**	leetroo
I'd like something...	**Želeo bih...**	zhehleho beeh...
sweet/sparkling/dry	**slatko/penušavo/oporo**	slahtko/pehnooshahvo/oporo
I want a bottle of white wine.	**Želeo bih flašu belog vina.**	zhehleho beeh flahshoo behlog veenah
I don't want anything too sweet.	**Ne želim slatko vino.**	neh zhehleem slahtko veeno
How much is a bottle of...?	**Koliko košta flaša...?**	koleeko koshtah flahshah

EATING OUT

That's too expensive.	**To je suviše skupo.**	to yeh sooveesheh skoopo
Haven't you anything cheaper?	**Zar nemate ništa jeftinije?**	zahr nehmahteh neeshtah yehfteeneeyeh
Fine, that will do.	**To sasvim odgovara.**	to sahsveem odgovahrah

If you enjoyed the wine, you may want to say:

Bring me another..., please.	**Donesite mi još jednu...molim Vas.**	donehseeteh mee yosh yehdnoo...moleem vahs
glass/bottle	**čašu/flašu**	chahshoo/flahshoo
What is the name of this wine?	**Kako se zove ovo vino?**	kahko seh zoveh ovo veeno
Where does this wine come from?	**Odakle je ovo vino?**	odahkleh yeh ovo veeno
How old is this wine?	**Koliko je staro ovo vino?**	koleeko yeh stahro ovo veeno

dry	**oporo**	oporo
red	**crno**	tserno
rosé	**ružica**	roozheetsah
sparkling	**penušavo**	pehnooshahvo
sweet	**slatko**	slahtko
white	**belo**	behlo
chilled	**rashladjeno**	rahshlahjehno
at room temperature	**na sobnoj temperaturi**	nah sobnoy tehmpehrahtooree

EATING OUT

Although there are certain principles concerning the choice of wine with a dish, it still remains a matter of personal preference. It is true that, on the whole, white wine goes better with fish or light meat; red, with dark meat. But it's your holiday, your palate – so choose what you (and your guests) want. Yugoslavia offers ample opportunity for this.

Other alcoholic drinks

Don't expect to find mixed drinks or cocktails in a small *gostiona* (gosteeonah). For these you'll have to go to more sophisticated bars and hotels.

I'll have a(n) ..., please.	**Molim Vas...**	moleem vahs
aperitif	**aperitiv**	ahpehreeteev
brandy (cognac)	**konjak**	koñahk
gin	**džin**	jeen
gin and tonic	**džin i tonik**	jeen ee toneek
gin-fizz	**džin fis**	jeen fees
liqueur	**liker**	leekehr
port	**port**	port
rum	**rum**	room
sherry	**šeri**	shehree
dry/sweet	**opor/slatki**	opor/slahtkee
vermouth	**vermut**	vehrmoot
vodka	**votku**	votkoo
whisky	**viski**	veeskee
whisky and soda	**viski sa sodom**	veeskee sah sodom

glass	**čaša**	chahshah
bottle	**flaša**	flahshah
single	**jedna čaša**	yehdnah chahshah
double	**duplo**	dooplo

Yugoslav specialities

kajsijevača
(kahyseeyehvahchah)
apricot brandy

klekovača
(klehkovahchah)
plum brandy mixed with berries

lozovača
(lozovahchah)
grape brandy

maraskino
(mahrahskeenoh)
maraschino cherry liqueur

EATING OUT

mastika (**mah**steekah)	a liquor distilled from mastic herbs
pelinkovac (peh**leen**kovahts)	an absinth liqueur
prepečenica (prehpeh**cheh**neetsah)	extra strong plum brandy
rakija (rah**kee**yah)	a general term for all local hard liquor; still, if you order **rakija** you will generally be served a **šljivovica**
šljivovica (**shly**ee**vo**veetsah)	plum brandy
vinjak (**vee**ñahk)	local cognac

I would like to taste *vinjak*, please.	**Želeo bih da probam vinjak, molim Vas.**	**zheh**leho beeh dah **pro**bahm **vee**ñahk **mo**leem vahs
Are there any local specialities?	**Da li imate nekih lokalnih specijaliteta?**	dah lee **ee**mahteh **neh**keeh lo**kahl**neeh spehtseeyah-**lee**tehtah
Bring me a glass of *maraskino*, please.	**Donesite mi čašu maraskina, molim Vas.**	do**neh**seeteh mee **chah**shoo mahrah**skee**nah **mo**leem vahs

EATING OUT

> **ŽIVELI!**
> (**zhee**vehlee)
> CHEERS!

Other beverages

I'd like a...	Želeo bih...	zhehleho beeh
Have you any...?	Imate li...?	eemahteh lee
chocolate	čokoladu	chokolahdoo
coffee	kafu	kahfoo
cup of coffee	šoljicu kafe	sholyeetsoo kahfeh
coffee with cream	kafu sa	kahfoo sah
	nemućenim	nehmoochehneem
	šlagom	shlahgom
expresso coffee	espreso kafu	ehsprehso kahfoo
iced coffee	ajskafe	ahyskahfeh
fruit juice	voćni sok	vochnee sok
grapefruit	grepfrut	grehpfroot
lemon/orange	limun/	leemoo/orahnjahdoo
	orandžadu	
pineapple/tomato	ananas/paradajz	ahnahnahs/pahrahdahyz
lemonade	limunadu	leemoonahdoo
milk	mleko	mlehko
mineral water	mineralnu vodu	meenehrahlnoo vodoo
orangeade	oranžadu	orahnjahdoo
soda water	soda vodu	sodah vodoo
tea	čaj	chahyah
with milk/lemon	sa mlekom/	sah mlehkom/leemoonom
	limunom	
tonic water	tonik	toneek

Note: Almost every area in Yugoslavia has its own kind of mineral water. It is always sold in bottles. Flavours vary.

Tea and coffee

Tea in Yugoslavia is never served with milk but always either with lemon or a mediocre rum. When you order coffee, it's almost certain to be *turska kava* (**toor**skah **kah**vah) – the Turkish brew. Though it's quite strong, Turkish coffee is usually well blended. The coffee, water and sugar are all boiled together, then poured directly into the cup. Let it sit a minute so that the grounds can settle to the bottom, and then sip only half the cup. Expresso or American-brewed coffee are served only in some big, international hotels.

Eating light – Snacks

The Yugoslav *bife* (**bee**feh – a kind of snack bar) offers a more limited choice of menu than you may be accustomed to in snack bars at home. There is no equivalent to the American drugstore.

Since most of the snacks are on display, you will not need to say much more than:

I'll have one of those, please.	**Molim Vas jedno od onog.**	moleem vahs **yeh**dno od onog
Give me two of those and one of those.	**Dajte mi dve od onih i jedan od onih.**	**dah**yteh mee dveh od oneeh ee **yeh**dahn od oneeh
Not that one... The one over there.	**Ne taj...Onaj gore.**	neh tahy...onahy **go**reh
On the top shelf/on the shelf below.	**Na najgornjoj polici/na donjoj polici.**	nah **nahy**gorñoy poleetsee/ nah **do**ñoy poleetsee
to the left	**na levo**	nah **leh**vo
to the right	**na desno**	nah **deh**sno
above	**gore**	**go**reh
below	**dole**	**do**leh
Over there.	**Tamo.**	**tah**mo
I want a/an/some..., please.	**Želim...molim Vas.**	**zheh**leem...**mo**leem vahs
Do you have any...?	**Imate li...?**	**ee**mahteh lee
I'd like a/an/some...	**Želim...**	**zheh**leem
beefburger	**faširani šnicl**	fah**shee**rahnee shneetsl
biscuits	**keks**	kehks
bread	**hleb [kruh]**	hlehb [krooh]
butter	**puter**	**poo**tehr
cake	**kolač**	**ko**lahch
chocolate	**čokoladu**	choko**lah**doo
cookies	**keks**	kehks
hot dog	**viršle**	**veersh**leh
ice-cream	**sladoled**	**slah**dolehd
pastry	**kolače**	ko**lah**cheh
pie	**paštetu**	pah**shteh**too
roll	**kiflu [kajzericu]**	**kee**floo [kah**y**zehreetsoo]
salad	**salatu**	sah**lah**too

EATING OUT

sandwich	**sendvič**	**sehnd**veech
sweets	**slatkiše**	**slaht**keesheh
toast	**prepržen hleb [kruh]**	**preh**perzhehn hlehb [krooh]
waffles	**kekse**	**kehhk**seh
How much is that?	**Koliko to košta?**	ko**lee**ko to **kosh**tah

garlic	**beli luk**	**beh**lee look
mustard	**senf**	sehnf
pepper	**biber**	**bee**ber
salt	**so**	so
sugar	**šećer**	**sheh**chehr
vinegar	**sirće [ocat]**	**seer**cheh [otsaht]

Travelling around

Plane

Very brief – because at any airport you're sure to find someone who speaks English. But here are a few airborne expressions you may want to know…

Do you speak English?	**Da li govorite engleski?**	dah lee govoreeteh ehnglehskee
Is there a flight to…?	**Da li ima let za…?**	dah lee eemah leht zah
When's the next plane to…?	**Kad ima sledeći avion za…?**	kahd eemah slehdehchee ahveeon zah
Can I make a connection to…?	**Imam li vezu za…?**	eemahm lee vehzoo zah
I'd like a ticket to…	**Želeo bih kartu za…**	zhehleho beeh kahrtoo zah
What's the fare to…?	**Koliko košta karta do…?**	koleeko koshtah kahrtah do
single (one-way) return (roundtrip)	**u jednom pravcu povratna**	oo yehdnom prahvtsoo povrahtnah
What time does the plane take off?	**Kada poleće avion?**	kahdah polehcheh ahveeon
What time do I have to check in?	**Kad treba da se javim?**	kahd trehbah dah seh yahveem
What's the flight number?	**Koji je broj leta?**	koyee yeh broy lehtah
What time do we arrive?	**Kad stižemo?**	kahd steezhehmo

DOLAZAK	**POLAZAK**
ARRIVAL	DEPARTURE

TRAVELLING AROUND

Train

You're probably not going to spend a great deal of time travelling by train or standing in the railway station, so we shall confine ourselves to certain stock situations, presenting them in the order you're likely to encounter them.

If you're worried about railway tickets or timetables, go to a travel agency where they speak English, or see the *portir* (**por**teer) of your hotel.

On the main railway lines in Yugoslavia, trains are electric or diesel. They're generally on time.

Types of trains

Ekspresni voz * (ehk**spreh**snee voz)	This train stops only at the main stations; a supplement is required. For some express trains, advance booking is necessary.
Brzi voz * (**ber**zee voz)	This train stops at main stations only. It may be necessary to book seats in advance.
Putnički voz * (**poot**neechkee voz)	A local train stopping at all stations
Poslovni voz * (poslovnee voz)	A day train running between the major cities (Belgrade-Zagreb, for instance), leaving in the morning and coming back in the evening; very fast and comfortable
Šinobus (**shee**noboos)	A small diesel train used for short runs

* **Voz** (train) is the word used in Belgrade and the eastern part of the country. In Zagreb and the western part it's **vlak**.

To the railway station

Where's the railway station?	**Gde je železnička stanica?**	gdeh yeh **zheh**lehzneechkah **stah**neetsah
Taxi, please!	**Taksi, molim!**	**tahk**see moleem
Take me to the railway station.	**Odvezite me na železničku stanicu.**	odvehzeeteh meh nah zhehlehzneechkoo **stah**neetsoo
What's the fare?	**Koliko košta?**	koleeko koshtah

Tickets

Where's the...?	**Gde je...?**	gdeh yeh
information office	**šalter za informacije**	**shahl**tehr zah eenformahtseeyeh
reservation office	**biro za rezervaciju karata**	**beero** zah rehzehrvahtseeyoo **kah**rahtan
ticket office	**prodaja karta**	prodahyah **kahr**tah
I want a ticket to Rijeka, second-class return.	**Želeo bih povratnu kartu za Rijeku, drugi razred.**	**zheh**leho beeh povrah tnoo **kahr**too zah **reey**ehkoo droogee rahzrehd
I'd like two singles to Dubrovnik.	**Želeo bih dve jednosmerne karte za Dubrovnik.**	**zheh**leho beeh dveh yehdnosmehrneh **kahr**teh zah **doo**brovneek
How much is the fare to Belgrade?	**Koliko košta karta za Beograd?**	koleeko koshtah **kahr**ta zah behograhd
Is it half price for a child?	**Da li se za dete plaća pola karte?**	dah lee seh zah **deh**teh plahchah polah **kahr**teh

Note: In Yugoslavia, children up to the age of four travel free; from four to twelve it's half price.

Possible answers	
Prvu ili drugu klasu?	First or second class?
U jednom pravcu ili povratnu kartu?	Single or return (one-way or roundtrip)?
Pola karte je do dvanaest godina.	It's half price up to the age of 12.
Moraćete da platite celu kartu.	You'll have to pay full fare.

FOR TAXI, see page 27

TRAVELLING AROUND

Further enquiries

Is it a through train?	Da li je to direktni voz*?	dah lee yeh to deerehktnee voz
Does this train stop at...?	Da li voz* staje u...?	dah lee voz stahyeh oo
When's the...train to Split?	Kad ide...voz* za Split?	kahd eedeh...voz zah spleet
first/last/next	prvi/poslednji/ sledeći	pervee/poslehdñee/ slehdehchee
What time does the train from Belgrade arrive?	Kad stiže voz* iz Beograda?	kahd steezheh voz eez behograhda
What time does the train for Sarajevo leave?	Kad polazi voz* za Sarajevo?	kahd polahzee voz zah sahrahyehvo
Will the train leave on time?	Da li voz* polazi na vreme?	dah lee voz polahzee nah vrehmeh
Is the train late?	Da li voz* kasni?	dah lee voz kahsnee
Is there a dining-car on the train?	Da li voz* ima kola za ručavanje?	dah lee voz eemah kolah zah roochahvahñeh

ULAZ	ENTRANCE
IZLAZ	EXIT
PERONI	TO THE PLATFORMS

Where's the...?

Where's the...?	Gde je...?	gdeh yeh
bar	bar	bahr
buffet	bife	beefeh
restaurant	restoran	rehstorahn
left luggage office	garderoba	gahrdehrobah
lost and found office	biro za nadjene stvari	beero zah nahjehneh stvahree
newsstand	kiosk za novine	keeosk zah noveeneh
waiting room	čekaonica	chehkahoneetsah
Where are the toilets?	Gde je toalet?	gdeh yeh toahleht

* **Vlak** in Zagreb and the western part of the country.

Platform (track)

What platform does the train for Rijeku leave from?	**Sa koga koloseka polazi voz* za Rijeku?**	sah **kogah kolosehkah polahzee voz reeyehkoo**
What platform does the train from Zagreb arrive at?	**Na koji kolosek dolazi voz* iz Zagreba?**	nah **koyee kolosehk dolahzee voz eez zah**grehbah
Where's platform 7?	**Gde je peron 7?**	gdeh yeh **pehron sehdahm**
Is this the right platform for the train to...?	**Da li je ovo peron za voz* za...?**	dah lee yeh ovo **pehron** zah voz zah

---

Possible answers

Ovo je direktni voz*.	It's a direct train.
Morate presedati u...	You have to change at...
Presednite u...u lokalni voz*.	Change at...and get a local train.
Peron...je...	Platform...is...
tamo/dole na levo/na desno	over there/downstairs on the left/on the right
Voz* za...kreće u...sa ...perona.	The train to...will leave at... from platform...
Voz* u...za...kasni... minuta.	The...train for...will be... minutes late.
Voz* iz...je upravo stigao na...peron.	The train from...is now arriving at platform...
Voz* kasni...minuta.	There'll be a delay of... minutes.

* **Vlak** in Zagreb and the western part of the country.

All aboard

Excuse me. May I get by?	**Izvinite. Mogu li da prodjem?**	eezveeneeteh mogoo lee dah projehm
Is this seat taken?	**Da li je ovo mesto zauzeto?**	dah lee yeh ovo mehsto zahoozehto
Is this seat free?	**Da li je ovo mesto slobodno?**	dah lee yeh ovo mehsto slobodno

> **ZABRANJENO PUŠENJE**
> NO SMOKING

I think that's my seat.	**Mislim da je to moje mesto.**	meesleem dah yeh to moyeh mehsto
Can you tell me when we get to...?	**Možete li mi reći kad stižemo u...?**	mozhehteh mee rehchee kahd steezhehmo oo
What station is this?	**Koja je ovo stanica?**	koyah yeh ovo stahneetsah
How long does the train stop here?	**Koliko dugo stoji voz [vlak] ovde?**	koleeko doogo stoyee voz [vlahk] ovdeh
When do we get to Titograd?	**Kad stižemo u Titograd?**	kahd steezhehmo oo teetograhd

Some time on the journey the ticket-collector (*kondukter–* kon**dook**tehr) will come around and say: *Karte molim* (Tickets, please).

Eating

If you want a full meal in the dining-car (*vagon-restoran —* **vah**gon rehs**toh**rahn), you may have to get a ticket from the attendant who'll come to your compartment. There are usually two sittings for lunch and dinner. State which one you prefer.

First/Second sitting, please.	**Prvu/Drugu partiju [prvo/drugo serviranje], molim.**	pervoo/droogoo pahrteeyoo [pervo/droogo sehrveerahñeh] moleem

TRAVELLING AROUND

Sleeping

Are there any free compartments in the sleeping car?	**Da li ima slobodnih kupea u kolima za spavanje?**	dah lee **ee**mah **slo**bodneeh koopehah oo koleemah zah **spah**vahñeh
Where's the sleeping car?	**Gde su kola za spavanje?**	gdeh soo **ko**lah zah **spah**vahñeh
Compartments 18 and 19, please.	**Kupe 18 i 19, molim.**	koo**peh** 18 ee 19 moleem
Would you make up our berths?	**Hoćete li napraviti naše krevete?**	hochehteh lee **nah**prahveetee **nah**sheh **kreh**vehteh
Would you call me at 7 o'clock?	**Probudite me, molim Vas, u sedam sati.**	pro**boo**deeteh meh moleem vahs oo **seh**dahm **sah**tee
Would you bring me some coffee/tea in the morning?	**Donesite mi, molim Vas, kafu/čaj ujutro.**	doneh**see**teh mee moleem vahs **kah**foo/chahy **oo**yootro

Baggage and porters

Can you help me with my bags?	**Možete li mi poneti kofere?**	mo**zheh**teh lee mee po**neh**tee **ko**fehreh
Put them down here, please.	**Stavite ih ovde, molim Vas.**	**stah**veeteh eeh **ov**deh **mo**leem vahs

Note: You could, if you want, have them sent *mitgepek* (**meet**-gehpehk). In that case, your luggage is put into the baggage car, and you collect it at the end of the trip, but there's an extra charge for this.

FOR PORTERS, see also page 24

TRAVELLING AROUND

Lost!

We hope you'll have no need for the following phrases on your trip... but just in case:

Where's the lost property office?	**Gde je biro za nadjene stvari?**	gdeh yeh beero zah nahjehneh stvahree
I've lost my...	**Izgubio sam...**	eezgoobeeo sahm
this morning	**jutros**	yootros
yesterday	**jučer**	yoochehr
I lost it in...	**Izgubio sam u...**	eezgoobeeo sahm oo
It's very valuable.	**To je vrlo skupoceno.**	to yeh verlo skoopotsehno

Timetables

If you intend to do a lot of train travelling, it might be a good idea to buy a timetable. These are based on the 24-hour clock and are for sale at ticket offices, information desks and in some bookshops.

I'd like to buy a timetable.	**Želeo bih da kupim red vožnje.**	zhehleho beeh dah koopeem rehd vozhñeh

Boats

Boats ply up and down the Danube. A river-boat trip on the Belgrade-Djerdap stretch of the Danube, with its medieval castles, vineyards and numerous points of interest (Tabula Traiana, for instance), is well worthwhile.

The phrases contained in the "Train" section will suffice for a river journey, so we'll content ourselves with learning just a few words:

berth	**ležaj**	lehzhahy
cabin	**kabina**	kahbeenah
deck	**paluba**	pahloobah
dock	**pristati**	preestahtee
port	**pristanište**	preestahneeshteh

Bus – Tramway (streetcar)

In most buses and tramways, you pay as you enter. In some rural buses, you may find the driver also acting as the conductor.

I'd like a bus pass.	Želeo bih pretplatnu kartu za autobus.	zhehleho beeh prehtplahtnoo kahrtoo zah ahootoboos
Where can I get a bus to...?	Gde mogu da uzmem autobus za...?	gdeh mogoo dah oozmehm ahootoboos zah
What bus do I take for...?	Koji autobus treba da uzmem za...?	koyee ahootoboos trehbah dah oozmehm zah
Where's the...?	Gde je...?	gdeh yeh
bus stop/bus station/ terminus	autobusna stanica/ poslednja stanica	ahootoboosnah stahneetsah/ poslehdñah stahneetsah
When's the...bus to Dubrovnik?	Kad ide...autobus za Dubrovnik?	kahd eedeh...ahootoboos zah doobrovneek
first/last/next	prvi/poslednji/ sledeći	pervee/poslehdñee/ slehdehchee
How often do the buses to Titograd run?	Kako često ide autobus za Titograd?	kahko chehsto eedeh ahootoboos zah teetograhd
How much is the fare to...?	Koliko košta do...?	koleeko koshtah do
Do I have to change buses?	Da li treba da menjam autobus?	dah lee trehbah dah mehñahm ahootoboos
How long does the journey take?	Koliko traje vožnja?	koleeko trahyeh vozhñah
Will you tell me when to get off?	Hoćete li mi, molim Vas, reći kad treba da sidjem.	hochehteh lee mee moleem vahs rehchee kahd trehbah dah seejehm
I want to get off at Marsala Tita street.	Hoću da sidjem u Maršala Tita ulici.	hochoo dah seejehm oo mahrshahlah teetah ooleetsee
Please let me off at the next stop.	Hteo bih da sidjem na sledećoj stanici, molim Vas.	hteho beeh dah seeyehm nah slehdehchoy stahneetsee moleem vahs

Your baggage will have to go on the roof/into the luggage compartment.	**Vaš prtljag se mora staviti na krov/na mesto za prtljag.**	vahsh pertlʸahg seh morah stahveetee nah krov/nah mehsto zah pertlʸahg
I want my baggage, please.	**Molim Vas moj prtljag.**	moleem vahs moy pertlʸahg

---

AUTOBUSKA STANICA
BUS STOP

STANICA PO POTREBI
STOP ON REQUEST

Or try one of these to get around...

bicycle	**bicikl [kotač]**	beetseekl [kotahch]
helicopter	**helikopter**	hehleekoptehr
hitch-hiking	**autostopiranje**	ahootostopeerahñeh
horseback riding	**jahanje**	yahhahñeh

And if you're really stuck, go...

walking	**pešice**	pehshitseh

Around and about – Sightseeing

Here we're more concerned with the cultural aspect of life than with entertainment; and, for the moment, with towns rather than the countryside. If you want a guide book, ask...

Can you recommend a good guide book for...?	**Možete li mi preporučiti dobar vodič za...?**	mozhehteh lee mee prehporoocheetee dobahr vodeech zah
Is there a tourist office?	**Ima li ovde turistički biro?**	eemah lee ovdeh tooreesteechkee beero
What are the main points of interest?	**Koja su mesta ovde najinteresantnija?**	koyah so mehstah ovdeh nahyeentehrehsahntneeyah
We're only here for...	**Ovde se zadržavamo samo...**	ovdeh seh zahderzhahvahmo sahmo
a few hours	nekoliko sati	nehkoleeko sahtee
a day	jedan dan	yehdahn dahn
three days	tri dana	tree dahnah
a week	nedelju dana	nehdehl'yo dahnah
Can you recommend a sightseeing tour?	**Da li mi možete preporučiti neku turu za razgledanje grada?**	dah lee mee mozhehteh prehporoocheetee nehkoo tooroo zah rahzglehdahñeh grahdah
Where does the bus start from?	**Odakle polazi autobus?**	odahkleh polahzee ahootoboos
Will it pick us up at the hotel?	**Da li nas može uzeti ispred hotela?**	dah lee nahs mozheh oozehtee eesprehd hotehlah
What bus/tram do we want?	**Koji autobus/ tramvaj nam treba?**	koyee ahootoboos trahmvahy nahm trehbah
Take a No. 7 from the Square.	**Uzmite broj sedam sa Trga.**	oozmeeteh broy sehdahm sah tergah
How much does the tour cost?	**Koliko košta obilazak?**	koleeko koshtah obeelahzahk
What time does the tour start?	**Kad počinje obilazak?**	kahd pocheeñeh obeelahzahk

SIGHTSEEING

FOR TIME OF DAY, see page 178

SIGHTSEEING

We'd like to rent a car for the day.	Želeo bih unajmiti kola za jedan dan.	zhehleho beeh eeznahymeetee kolah zah yehdahn dahn
Is there an English-speaking guide?	Da li ima vodič koji govori engleski?	dah lee eemah vodeech koyee govoree ehnglehskee
Where is/are the...?	Gde je/su...?	gdeh yeh/soo
abbey	manastir (samostan)	mahnahsteer (sahmostahn)
aquarium	akvarium	ahkvahreeoom
antiquities	starine	stahreeneh
art gallery	umetnička galerija	oomehtneechkah gahlehreeyah
botanical gardens	botanička bašta	botahneechkah bahshtah
building	zgrada	zgrahdah
business district	poslovni centar	poslovnee tsehntahr
castle	zamak	zahmahk
catacombs	katakombe	kahtahkombeh
cathedral	katedrala	kahtehdrahlah
cave	pećina (špilja)	pehcheenah (shpeelyah)
cemetery	groblje	groblyeh
church	crkva	tsehrkvah
concert hall	koncertna dvorana	kontsehrtnah dvorahnah
convent	samostan	sahmostahn
docks	brodski dokovi	brodskee dokovee
downtown area	centar grada	tsehntahr grahdah
exhibition	izložba	eezlozhbah
factory	tvornica	tvorneetsah
fortress	tvrdjava	tverjahvah
fountain	vodoskok	vodoskok
gardens	vrtovi	verto vee
glass-works	tvornica stakla	tvorneetsah stahklah
harbour	luka	lookah
lake	jezero	yehzehro
law courts	sud	sood
library	biblioteka	beebleeotehkah
market	pijaca	peeyahtsah
memorial	spomenik	spomehneek
monastery	manastir	mahnahsteer
monument	spomenik	spomehneek
mosque	džamija	jahmeeyah
museum	muzej	moozehy
observatory	opservatorija	opsehrvahtoreeyah
opera house	opera	opehrah
park	park	pahrk
planetarium	planetarium	plahnehtahreeoom

(central) post office	(glavna) pošta	(glahvnah) poshtah
ruins	razvaline	rahzvahleeneh
shopping centre	centar za kupovinu	tsehntar zah koopoveenoo
shrine	grobnica	grobneetsah
stadium	stadion	stahdeeon
statue	spomenik	spomehneek
synagogue	sinagoga	seenahgogah
television studios	televizijski studio	tehlehveezeeyskee stoodeeo
temple	hram	hrahm
tomb	grobnica	grobneetsah
tower	toranj	torahñ
town centre	centar grada	tsehntar grahdah
town hall	opština grada (većnica)	opshteenah grahdah (vehchneetsah)
university	univerzitet	ooneevehrzeeteht
vineyards	vinogradi	veenograhdee
zoo	zoološki vrt	zooloshkee vert

Admission

Is the...open on Sundays?	Da li je...otvoreno nedeljom?	dah lee yeh...otvorehno nehdehlyom
When does it open?	Kad se otvara?	kahd seh otvahrah
When does it close?	Kad se zatvara?	kahd seh zahtvahrah
How much is the admission charge?	Koliko košta ulaz?	koleeko koshtah oolahz
Is there any reduction for students?	Imaju li studenti popust?	eemahyoo lee stoodehntee popoost
Here's my ticket.	Izvolite moju kartu.	eezvoleeteh moyoo kahrtoo
Have you a guide book (in English)?	Imate li vodič (na engleskom)?	eemahteh lee vodeech (nah ehnglehskom)
Is it all right to take pictures?	Da li je dozvoljeno fotografisanje?	dah lee yeh dozvolyehno fotografeesahñeh

ULAZ SLOBODAN   ADMISSION FREE

SIGHTSEEING

Who – What – When?

What's that building?	Kakva je to zgrada?	kahkvah yeh to zgrahdah
Who was the...?	Ko je bio...?	ko yeh beeo
architect	arhitekta	ahrheetehktah
artist	umetnik	oomehtneek
painter	slikar	sleekahr
sculptor	skulptor	skoolptor
Who built it?	Ko je to sagradio?	ko yeh to sahgrahdeeo
Who painted that picture?	Ko je naslikao tu sliku?	ko yeh nahsleekaho too sleekoo
When did he live?	Kada je on živeo?	kahdah yeh on zheeveho
When was it built?	Kada je to sagradjeno?	kahdah yeh to sahgrahjehno
Where's the house where...lived?	Gde je kuća u kojoj je živeo...?	gdeh yeh koochah oo koyoy yeh zheeveho
We're interested in...	Nas interesuje...	nahs eentehrehsooyeh
antiques	starine	stahreeneh
archaeology	arheologija	ahrhehologeeyah
art	umetnost	oomehtnost
botany	botanika	botahnkah
ceramics	keramika	kehrahmeekah
coins	stari novac	stahree novahts
fine arts	umetnost	oomehtnost
furniture	nameštaj	nahmehshtahy
geology	geologija	gehologeeyah
history	istorija [povijest]	eestoreeyah [poveeyehst]
local crafts	lokalne rukotvorine	lokahlneh rookotvoreeneh
medicine	medicina	mehdeetseenah
music	muzika	moozeekah
natural history	prirodopis	preerodopees
ornithology	nauka o pticama	nahookah o pteetsahmah
painting	slikarstvo	sleekahrstvo
pottery	grnčarija	gernchahreeyah
sculpture	skulptura	skoolptoorah
zoology	zoologija	zoologeeyah
Where's the... department?	Gde je odsek...?	gdeh yeh odsehk

Just the adjective you've been looking for...

It's...	To je...	to yeh
amazing	zapanjujuće	zahpahñooyoocheh
awful	strašno	strahshno
beautiful	divno	deevno
gloomy	sumorno	soomorno
hideous	grozno	grozno
interesting	interesantno	eentehrehsahntno
magnificent	krasno	krahsno
monumental	veličanstveno	vehleechahnstvehno
overwhelming	neodoljivo	nehodolʲeevo
sinister	rdjavo	erjahvo
strange	čudno	choodno
superb	izvanredno	eezvahnrehdno
terrible	strašno	strahshno
terrifying	užasno	oozhahsno
ugly	ružno	roozhno
vivid	živo	zheevo

Church services

All churches and cathedrals are open to the public. Some are, however, not open all day long. In most churches it is not necessary to ask permission for taking photographs.

Is there a...near here?	Ima li...ovde?	eemah lee...ovdeh
Orthodox church	pravoslavna crkva	prahvoslahvnah tsehrkvah
Protestant church	protestantska crkva	protehstahntskah tsehrkvah
Catholic church	katolička crkva	kahtoleechkah tserkvah
synagogue	sinagoga	seenahgogah
mosque	džamija	jahmeeyah

At what time is the...?	U koliko sati je...?	oo koleeko sahtee yeh
morning liturgy	jutarnja liturgija	yootahrñah leetoorgeeyah
morning/evening services	jutarnja/večernja služba	yootahrñah/vehchehrñah sloozhbah
high mass	svečana misa	svehchahnah meesah
sabbath services	subotnja služba	soobotñah sloozhbah

Where can I find... who speaks English?	Gde mogu da nadjem...koji govori engleski?	gdeh mogoo dah nahyehm... koyee govoree ehnglehskee
a clergyman	sveštenika	svehshtehneekah
a rabbi	rabina	rahbeenah

SIGHTSEEING

Relaxing

Cinema (movies) – Theatre

Cinema showings are not continuous in Yugoslavia. Tickets can generally be obtained just before the performance starts; sometimes, however, you may need to book your seat in advance. You can expect one feature film, a newsreel, and some advertisements. There's no intermission midway through the feature. Smoking is not allowed, either in cinemas or in theatres. The first cinema showing generally starts at 2 or 3 p.m. At some cinemas thare are performances beginning at 10 a.m. Theatres start at 8 p.m. Booking in advance is advisable for new films and plays.

You can find out what's playing from daily newspapers and billboards. In some large towns, you can buy publications of the type "This week in…".

Have you a copy of "This week in…"?	Imate li jedan primerak publi- kacije "Ovo nedelje u…"?	eemahteh lee yehdahn preemehrahk poobleekah- tseeyeh oveh nehdehl'eh oo
What's on at the cinema tonight?	Šta se daje u kinu večeras?	shtah seh dahyeh oo keenoo vehchehrahs
What's playing at the National Theatre?	Šta se daje u Narodnom pozorištu [kazalištu]	shtah seh dahyeh oo nahrodnom pozoreeshtoo [kahzahleeshtoo]
What sort of film is it?	Kakav je to film?	kahkahv yeh to feelm
Who's it by?	Ko igra?	ko eegrah
Can you recommend a…?	Možete li mi preporučiti…?	mozhehteh lee mee prehporoocheetee
comedy	komediju	komehdeeyoo
drama	dramu	drahmoo
film	film	feelm
musical	mjuzikl	myoozeekl
play	komad	komahd
revue	reviju	rehveeyoo
thriller	kriminalni film	kreemeenahlnee feelm
western	kaubojski film	kahbooyskee feelm

At what theatre is that new play by... showing?	U kome pozorištu [kazalištu] se daje onaj novi komad od...?	oo komeh pozoreeshtoo [kahzahleeshtoo] seh dahyeh onahy novee komahd od
Where's that new film by... playing?	Gde se daje onaj novi film od...?	gdeh seh dahyeh onahy novee feelm od
Who's in it?	Ko igra?	ko eegrah
Who's playing the lead?	Ko igra glavnu ulogu?	ko eegrah glahvnoo oologoo
Is the dialogue in Serbo-Croatian?	Da li je film na srpskohrvatskom	dah lee yeh feelm nah serpskohervahtskom
What time does it begin	U koliko sati počinje?	oo koleeko sahtee pocheeñeh
What time does the show end?	Kad se predstava završava?	kahd seh prehdstahvah zahvershahvah
Is there a matinee*/ late show?	Da li ima matine*/ predstava kasno uveče?	dah lee eemah mahteeneh/ prehdstahvah kahsno oovehcheh
What time does the first evening performance start?	Kad počinje prva večernja predstava?	kahd pocheeneh pervah vehcherñah prehdstahvah
Are there any tickets for tonight?	Ima li još karata za večeras?	eemah lee yosh kahrahtah zah vehchehrahs
I want to reserve two tickets for the show on Friday evening.	Želim da rezervišem dve karte za pretstavu u petak uveče.	zhemleem dah rehzhehrveeshehm dveh kahrteh zah prehdstahvoo oo pehtahk oovehcheh
Can I have a ticket for the matinee* on Tuesday?	Mogu li da dobijem kartu za matine* u utorak?	mogoo lee dah dobeeyehm kahrtoo zah mahteeneh oo ootorahk
I want a seat in the stalls (orchestra).	Želim jednu kartu u parteru.	zhehleem yehdnoo kahrtoo oo pahrtehroo
Not too far back.	Ne suviše nazad.	neh sooveesheh nahzahd
Somewhere in the middle.	Negde u sredini.	nehgdeh oo srehdeenee
What are the cheapest seats in the balcony?	Koja su najjeftinija sedišta na balkonu?	koyah soo nahyyehfteeneeyah sehdeeshtah nah bahlkonoo

* Careful: in some places in Yugoslavia, matine means a morning performance beginning at 10 or 10.30.

RELAXING

May I have a programme, please?	**Molim Vas jedan program.**	moleem vahs **yeh**dahn **prog**rahm
Can I check this coat?	**Mogu li ostaviti ovaj kaput u garderobu?**	mogoo lee ostah**vee**tee **ov**ahy **kah**poot oo **gahr**dehroboo
Here's my ticket.	**Izvolite kartu.**	eez**vo**leeteh **kahr**too

Opera – Ballet – Concert

Where's the opera house?	**Gde je opera?**	gdeh yeh **op**ehrah
Where's the concert hall?	**Gde je koncertna dvorana?**	gdeh yeh kont**sehrt**naah dvo**rah**nah
What's on at the opera tonight?	**Šta se daje večeras u operi?**	shtah seh **dah**yeh veh**cheh**rahs oo **op**ehree
Who's singing?	**Ko peva?**	ko **peh**vah
Who's dancing?	**Ko igra?**	ko **ee**grah
What time does the performance start?	**Kad počinje predstava?**	kahd po**chee**ñeh **prehd**stahvah
What orchestra is playing?	**Koji orkestar svira?**	**koy**ee or**keh**stahr **svee**ran
What are they playing?	**Šta sviraju?**	shtah **svee**rahyoo
Who's the conductor?	**Ko je dirigent?**	ko yeh deeree**gehnt**

RELAXING

Possible answers

Žao mi je, sve je rasprodano.	I'm sorry, we're sold out.
Imamo još nekoliko slobodnih mesta na balkonu levo.	There are only a few seats in the circle (balcony) left.
Vaše karte molim.	Your ticket, please.
Ovo je Vaše mesto.	This is your seat.

Note: Usherettes are not tipped in Yugoslavia.

Nightclubs – Discotheques

The late-sleeping tourist will have no cause for complaint. He can find sophisticated nightclubs in some of the bigger luxury hotels, while a fishing village may surprise him with a discotheque full of jostling jitterbugs. Travel agencies operate night cruises aboard floating dance palaces plying the Adriatic.

The sign *Bar* indicates a nightclub (bars are called *bife*).

Can you recommend a good nightclub	**Možete li mi preporučiti dobar bar?**	mozhehteh lee mee prehporoocheetee dobahr bahr
Is there a floor show?	**Da li ima program?**	dah lee eemah prograhm
What time does the floor show begin?	**Kad počinje program?**	kahd pocheeñeh prograhm
Is evening dress necessary?	**Da li je večernje odelo neophodno?**	dah lee yeh vehchehrñeh odehlo nehophodno

And once inside…

A table for two, please.	**Sto za dvoje, molim.**	sto zah dvoyeh moleem
My name is…I reserved a table for four.	**Ja se zovem… Rezervisao sam sto za četiri osobe.**	yah seh zovehm… rehzehrveesaho sahm sto zah chehteeree osobeh
I telephoned you earlier.	**Telefonirao sam Vam ranije.**	tehlehfoneeraho sahm vahm rahneeyeh
We haven't got a reservation.	**Mi nemamo rezervaciju.**	mee nehmahmo rehzehrvahtseeyoo

RELAXING

Dancing

Where can we go dancing?	**Gde možemo da idemo na ples?**	gdeh mozhehmo dah eedehmo nah plehs
Is there a dance hall anywhere here?	**Da li ovde negde ima diskoteka?**	dah lee ovdeh nehgdeh eemah deeskotehkah
There is a ball at the...	**U...je bal.**	oo...yeh bahl
Would you like to dance?	**Da li biste hteli da plešete?**	dah lee beesteh htehlee dah plehshehteh
May I have this dance?	**Smem li Vas moliti za ovaj ples?**	smehm lee vahs moleetee zah ovahy plehs

Do you happen to play...?

On rainy days, this page may solve your problems...

Do you happen to play chess?	**Da li možda igrate šah?**	dah lee mozhdah eegrahteh shah
I'm afraid I don't.	**Nažalost ne.**	nahzhahlost neh
Yes, I'd like a game.	**Da. Rado bih odigrao jednu partiju.**	dah. rahdo beeh odeegraho yehdnoo pahrteeyoo
No, but I'll give you a game of draughts (checkers).	**Ne, ali mogu da odigram partiju dame.**	neh ahlee mogoo dah odeegrahm pahrteeyoo dahmeh
king	**kralj**	krahlʸ
queen	**kraljica [dama]**	krahlʸveetsah [dahmah]
castle (rock)	**top [kula]**	top [koolah]
bishop	**lovac**	lovahts
knight	**konj [skakač]**	koñ [skahkahch]
pawn	**pion [pešak]**	peeon [pehshahk]
Checkmate!	**Šahmat!**	shahmaht
Do you play cards?	**Da li igrate karte?**	dah lee eegrahteh kahrteh
bridge	**bridž**	breej
whist	**vist**	veest
poker	**poker**	pokehr

RELAXING

spades	**pik**	peek
hearts	**herc**	hehrts
diamonds	**karo**	kahro
clubs	**tref**	trehf

ace	**as**	ahs
king	**kralj**	krahlʸ
queen	**kraljica [dama]**	krahlʸeetsah [dahmah]
jack	**pub**	poob
joker	**džoker**	jokehr

People don't generally play cards in Yugoslavian pubs. Chess is more common, as well as dominoes and draughts. Slot machines and other mechanical games may be encountered, but not often. You may want to say:

| What are you playing? | **Šta igrate?** | shtah eegrahteh |

Casino

You'll find a casino at some major resorts and larger cities in Yugoslavia. Most stay open all year, but the normal season, particularly at the seaside, runs from late spring until October. To get into a casino, you'll need your passport. You must also have a "clean record" in the gambling world. For your part, you need have no doubts about the honesty of the game. All legitimate casinos are strictly controlled and regularly inspected. Casinos are anxious to avoid any risk of scandal or adverse public relations.

The language of the casino is mostly English, French or German. The croupiers will know enough of these languages for your requirements.

RELAXING

Sports

A list of popular sports in Yugoslavia would include football (soccer), basketball, handball (European style), winter sports and all water sports. Tennis isn't a major sport in Yugoslavia but courts do exist at certain hotels as well as tennis clubs.

Is there a football (soccer) match anywhere this Saturday?	**Da li negde ima fudbalska utakmica ove subote?**	dah lee **neh**gdeh **ee**mah **food**bahlskah **oo**tahkmeetsah oveh **soo**boteh
Who's playing?	**Ko igra?**	ko **ee**grah
I'd like to see a boxing match.	**Želim da vidim jedan boks meč.**	**zheh**leem dah **vee**deem **yeh**dahn boks mehch
Can you get me a couple of tickets?	**Možete li mi nabaviti dve karte?**	**mozh**ehteh mee **nah**bahveetee dveh **kahr**teh
Where's the nearest golf course?	**Gde je najbliže igralište za golf?**	gdeh yeh **nah**bleezheh **ee**grahleeshteh zah golf
Can we hire (rent) clubs?	**Možemo li unajmiti štapove za golf?**	**mozh**ehmo lee **oo**nahymeetee **shtah**poveh zah golf
Where are the tennis courts?	**Gde su teniska igrališta?**	gdeh soo **teh**neeskah **ee**grahleeshtah
What's the charge per...?	**Koliko košta na...?**	ko**lee**ko **ko**shtah nah
hour/day/round	**sat/dan/partiju**	saht/dahn/**pahr**teeyoo
Where's the nearest race course (racetrack)?	**Gde je najbliže trkalište?**	gdeh yeh **nah**bleezheh **ter**kahleeshteh
What's the admission charge?	**Koliko košta ulaz?**	ko**lee**ko **ko**shtah **oo**lahz
Is there a swimming pool here?	**Ima li ovde bazen za plivanje?**	**ee**mah lee **ov**deh **bah**zehn zah **plee**vahñeh
Is it open-air or indoor?	**Da li je otvoren ili zatvoren?**	dah lee yeh **ot**vorehn **ee**lee **zaht**vorehn
Is it heated?	**Da li se greje?**	dah lee seh **greh**yeh
Can one swim in the lake?	**Da li se može plivati u jezeru?**	dah lee seh **mozh**eh **plee**vahtee oo **yeh**zehroo

Fishing

Getting a short-term fishing permit is fairly simple in Yugoslavia. The best thing to do is to ask for information from the local harbour authorities or at an information office because the regulations vary from one place to another.

Is there any good fishing around here?	**Da li ovde negde ima neko dobro mesto za pecanje?**	dah lee ovdeh nehgdeh eemah nehko dobro mehsto zah pehtsahñeh
Do I need a permit?	**Da li mi treba dozvola?**	dah lee mee trehbah dozvolah
Where can I get one?	**Gde je mogu dobiti?**	gdeh yeh mogoo dobeetee

Hunting

Is the hunting season open?	**Da li je sezona lova otvorena?**	dah lee yeh sehzonah lovah otvorehnah
I'd like to hire a horse and riding equipment.	**Hteo bih da unajmim konja i jahaću opremu.**	hteho beeh dah oonahymeem koñah ee yahhahchoo oprehmoo
big game	**krupna divljač**	kroopnah deevlʸanch
fox	**lisica**	leeseetsah
bear	**medved**	mehdvehd
deer	**jelen**	yehlehn
wild duck	**divlje patke**	deevlʸeh pahtkeh
boar	**vepar**	vehpahr

On the beach

Is it safe for swimming?	**Da li je bezbedno za plivanje?**	dah lee yeh behzbehdno zah pleevahñeh
Is there a lifeguard?	**Da li ima spasilačka služba?**	dah lee eemah spahseelahchkah sloozhbah
Is it safe for children?	**Da li je bezbedno za decu?**	dah lee yeh behzbehdno zah dehtsoo
No, not today. The red flag's up. *	**Ne, danas nije. Crvena zastava je dignuta.**	neh dahnahs neeyeh. tservehnah zahstahvah yeh deegnootah

* A red flag or some other signal is flown when the sea is considered dangerous.

RELAXING

Are there any dangerous currents?	Da li ima opasnih struja?	dah lee **ee**mah o**pah**sneeh **stroo**yah
What's the temperature of the water?	Kakva je temperatura vode?	**kahk**vah yeh tehmpehrah-**too**rah **vo**deh
I want to hire a/an/some...	Hteo (Htela*) bih da unajmim...	**hte**ho (**hteh**lah) beeh dah oo**nah**ymeem
air mattress	dušek za vodu	**doo**shehk zah **vo**doo
bathing hut (cabana)	kabinu	kah**bee**noo
deck chair	ligeštul	**lee**gehshtool
skin-diving equipment	opremu za ronjenje	**o**prehmoo zah **ro**ñehñeh
sunshade	suncobran	**soont**sobrahn
water skis	skije za vodu	**skee**yeh zah **vo**doo
Where can I rent a canoe?	Gde mogu da unajmim čamac?	gdeh **mo**goo dah oo**nah**ymeem **chah**mahts
motor boat	motorni čamac	mo**tor**nee **chah**mahts
rowing boat	čamac na vesla	**chah**mahts nah **veh**slah
sailing boat	jedrilicu	yeh**dree**leetsoo
paddle boat	čamac sa pedalama	**chah**mahts sah peh**dah**lahmah
What's the charge?	Koliko košta?	ko**lee**ko **kosh**tah

PRIVATNA PLAŽA
PRIVATE BEACH

KUPANJE ZABRANJENO
NO BATHING

I'd like to go to a skating rink.	Hteo bih da idem na klizalište.	**hte**ho beeh dah **ee**dehm nah **klee**zahleeshteh
Is there one near here?	Da li ima neko ovde u blizini?	dah lee **ee**mah **neh**ko **ov**deh oo **blee**zeenee
What are the skiing conditions like at...?	Kakvi su uslovi za skijanje u...?	**kahk**vee soo **oo**slovee zah **skee**yahñeh oo
Can I take skiing lessons there?	Mogu li tamo da uzimam časove skijanja?	**mo**goo lee **tah**mo dah oo**zee**mahm **chah**so veh **skee**yahñah
Is there a ski lift?	Da li ima uspinjača?	dah lee **ee**mah oospee**ñahch**ah
I want to rent some skates/skiing equipment.	Hteo bih da unajmim klizaljke/skijašku opremu.	**hte**ho beeh dah oo**nah**ymeem **klee**zahlʸkeh/**skee**yahshkoo **o**prehmoo

* Feminine. See grammar.

Camping – Countryside

In many parts of Yugoslavia, camping isn't allowed without
a permit. There are plenty of authorized camping sites, some
with very good facilities.

If you want to be on the safe side, choose a site recognized by
the AMSJ *(Auto Moto Savez Jugoslavije)*. There are quite a
few of them, particularly on the coast and in large cities.

If you want to camp on private land, get permission from the
owner first.

Can we camp here?	**Možemo li ovde kampovati?**	mozhehmo lee ovdeh kahmpovahtee
Is there a camping site near here?	**Da li ima kamp u blizini?**	dah lee eemah kahmp oo bleezeenee
May we camp in your field?	**Možemo li kampovati na Vašem polju?**	mozhehmo lee kahmpovahtee nah vahshehm pol'oo
Can we park our caravan (trailer) here?	**Možemo li ovde parkirati našu prikolicu?**	mozhehmo lee ovdeh pahrkeerahtee nahshoo preekoleetsoo
Is this an official camping site?	**Da li je ovo javni kamping?**	dah lee yeh ovo yahvnee kahmpeeng
May we light a fire?	**Možemo li naložiti vatru?**	mozhehmo lee nahlozheetee vahtroo
Is there drinking water?	**Ima li vode za piće?**	eemah lee vodeh zah peecheh
What are the facilities?	**Kako je kamp opremljen?**	kahko yeh kahmp oprehml'ehn
Are there shopping facilities on the site?	**Da li ima prodavnica u kampu?**	dah lee eemah prodahvneetsah oo kahmpoo
Are there...?	**Ima li...?**	eemah lee
baths/showers/ toilets	**kupatila/tuševa/ toaleta**	koopahteelah/tooshehvah/ toahlehtah

Note: If you are a member of an international association of
campers, you can get considerable discounts in AMSJ camps.

90

What's the charge...?	**Koliko košta...?**	koleeko koshtah
per day	**na dan**	nah dahn
per night	**za jednu noć**	zah yehdnoo noch
per person	**po osobi**	po osobee
for a car	**za kola**	zah kolah
for a tent	**za šator**	zah shahtor
for a caravan (trailer)	**za prikolicu**	zah preekoleetsoo

KAMPOVANJE ZABRANJENO

CAMPING PROHIBITED

PRIKOLICE NICU DOZVOLJENE

NO CARAVANS (TRAILERS)

How far is it to...?	**Koliko ima do...?**	koleeko eemah do
Are we on the right road for...?	**Da li smo na pravom putu za...?**	dah lee smo nah prahvom pootoo zah
Where does this road lead to?	**Kuda vodi ovaj put?**	koodah vodee ovahy poot
Can you show us on the map where we are?	**Možete li nam pokazati na karti gde se nalazimo?**	mozhehteh lee nahm pokahzahteh nah kahrtee gdeh seh nahlahzeemo
Is there a youth hostel anywhere near here?	**Ima li negde ovde blizu omladinsko letovalište?**	eemah lee nehgdeh ovdeh bleezoo omlahdeensko lehtovahleeshteh
Is there any inexpensive accommodation near here?	**Ima li ovde neki jeftin smeštaj?**	eemah lee ovdeh nehkee yehfteenee smehshtahy
Do you know anyone who can put us up for the night?	**Da li znate nekog ko bi nas mogao smestiti preko noći?**	dah lee znahteh nehkog ko bee nahs mogao smehsteetee prehko nochee

Landmarks

barn	**žitnica [ambar]**	zheetneetsah [ahmbahr]
bridge	**most**	most
building	**zgrada**	zgrahdah
canal	**kanal**	kahnahl
brook	**potok**	potok
church	**crkva**	tserkvah
cliff	**klif**	kleef
cornfield	**polje sa žitom**	pol'yeh sah zheetom
cottage	**koliba**	koleebah
farm	**seosko imanje**	sehosko eemahñeh
field	**polje**	pol'yeh

footpath	**staza**	stahzah
forest	**šuma**	shoomah
hamlet	**zaseok**	zahsehok
heath	**pustara**	poostahrah
hill	**brežuljak**	brehzhoolʸahk
house	**kuća**	koochah
inn	**gostionica**	gosteeoneetsah
lake	**jezero**	yehzehro
marsh	**močvara**	mochvahrah
mountain	**planina**	plahneenah
path	**staza**	stahzah
plantation	**plantaža**	plahntahzhah
pond	**ribnjak**	reebñahk
river	**reka**	rehkah
road	**put [cesta]**	poot [tsehstah]
spring	**izvor**	eezvor
stream	**rečica [potok]**	rehcheetsah [potok]
swamp	**močvara**	mochvahrah
track	**staza**	stahzah
tree	**stablo**	stahblo
valley	**dolina**	doleenah
village	**selo**	sehlo
vineyard	**vinograd**	veenograhd
waterfall	**vodopad**	vodopahd
well	**bunar [izvor]**	boonahr [eezvor]
wood	**šuma**	shoomah

ZABRANJEN PROLAZ
NO TRESPASSERS

What's the name of that river?	**Kako se zove ta reka?**	kahko seh zoveh tah rehkah
How high are those hills?	**Koliko su visoki oni bregovi?**	koleeko soo veesokee onee brehgovee
Is there a scenic route to…?	**Ima li lep put do…?**	eemah lee lehp poot do

And if you're tired of walking, you can always try hitch-hiking (*ići autostopom*–**ee**chee **ah**ootostopom), though you may have to wait a long time for a lift.

Can you give me a lift to…?	**Možete li me povesti do…?**	mozhehteh lee meh povehstee do

CAMPING – COUNTRYSIDE

Making friends

You'll find it easy to start up a conversation with Yugoslavs, particularly when they learn you're a foreigner. As a matter of fact, they'll probably start the conversation first. Yugoslavs are accustomed to meeting foreigners and eager to help them. You'll find them hospitable as well as curious about your country.

Introductions

How do you do?	**Dobar dan.**	dobahr dahn
How are you?	**Kako ste?**	kahko steh
Fine, thanks. And you.	**Hvala dobro. A Vi?**	hvahlah dobro. ah vee
May I introduce Miss Philips?	**Dozvolite da Vam predstavim gospodjicu Philips.**	dozvoleeteh dah vahm prehdstahveem gospojeetsoo Philips
I'd like you to meet a friend of mine.	**Hteo bih Vam predstaviti svoga prijatelja.**	hteho beeh vahm prehdstahveetee svogah preeyahtehlʲah
John, this is...	**John, ovo je...**	John ovo yeh
My name's...	**Ja se zovem...**	yah seh zovehm
Delighted to meet you/Glad to know you.	**Drago mi je da sam Vas upoznao.**	drahgo mee yeh dah sahm vahs oopoznaho

Follow-up

How long have you been here?	**Koliko dugo ste ovde?**	koleeko doogo steh ovdeh
We've been here about a week.	**Ovde smo oko nedelju dana.**	ovdeh smo oko nehdehlʲoo dahnah
Is this your first visit?	**Da li ste ovde prvi put?**	dah lee steh ovdeh pervee poot

No, we came here last year.	**Ne, bili smo ovde prošle godine.**	neh beelee smo ovdeh proshleh godeeneh
Are you enjoying your stay?	**Da li Vam se ovde dopada?**	dah lee vahm seh ovdeh dopahdah
Yes, I like...very much.	**Da,...mi se dopada vrlo mnogo.**	dah...mee seh dopahdah verlo mnogo
Are you on your own?	**Da li ste sami?**	dah lee steh sahmee
I'm with...	**Ja sam sa...**	yah sahm sah
my wife	**svojom suprugom**	svoyom sooproogom
my family	**svojom porodicom**	svoyom porodeetsom
my parents	**svojim roditeljima**	svoyeem rodeetehl'eemah
some friends	**nekim prijateljima**	nehkeem preeyahtehl'eemah
Where do you come from?	**Odakle ste?**	odahkleh steh
What part of Yugoslavia do you come from?	**Iz koga dela Jugoslavije ste?**	eez kogah dehlah yoogoslahveeyeh steh
I'm from...	**Ja sam iz...**	yah sahm eez
Do you live here?	**Da li ovde živite?**	dah lee ovdeh zheeveeteh
I'm a student.	**Ja sam student/ studentkinja.**	yah sahm stoodehnt/ stoodehntkeeñah
What are you studying?	**Šta studirate?**	shtah stoodeerahteh
We're here on holiday.	**Ovde smo na odmoru.**	ovdeh smo nah odmoroo
I'm here on a business trip.	**Ovde sam poslovno.**	ovdeh sam poslovno
What kind of business are you in?	**U kojoj ste struci?**	oo koyoy steh strootsee
I hope we'll see you again soon.	**Nadam se da ćemo se uskoro opet videti.**	nahdahm seh dah chehmo seh ooskoro opeht veedehtee
See you later/ tomorrow.	**Videćemo se kasnije/sutra.**	veedehchehmo seh kahsneeyeh/sootrah
I'm sure we'll run into each other again some time.	**Sigurno ćemo se jedanput opet sresti.**	seegoorno chehmo seh yehdahnpoot opeht srehstee

Invitations

My wife and I would like you to dine with us on...	**Moja žena i ja bismo želeli da Vas pozovemo na večeru u...**	moyah zhehnah ee yah beesmo zhehlehlee dah vahs pozovehmo nah vehchehroo oo
We're giving a small party tomorrow night. I do hope you can come.	**Sutra uveče nam dolazi malo društvo. Nadam se da možete doći.**	sootrah oovehcheh nahm dolahzee mahlo drooshtvo. nahdahm seh dah mozhehteh dochee
Can you come round for cocktails this evening?	**Možete li doći večeras na koktel?**	mozhehteh lee dochee vehchehrahs nah koktehl
There's a party. Are you coming?	**Ima jedna zabava. Hoćete li doći?**	eemah yehdnah zahbahvah. hochehteh lee dochee
That's very kind of you.	**To je vrlo ljubazno od Vas.**	to yeh verlo l'oobahzno od vahs
I'd love to come.	**Rado bih došao (došla*).**	rahdo beeh doshaho (doshlah)
What time shall we come?	**Kad treba da dodjemo?**	kahd trehbah dah dojehmo
Can I bring a friend/ girl friend?	**Mogu li da dovedem jednog prijatelja/ prijateljicu?**	mogoo lee dah dovehdehm yehdnog preeyahtehl'ah/ preeyahtehl'eetsoo
There's no need to dress, is there?	**Nije potrebno da se specijalno obučem, zar ne?**	neeyeh potrehbno dah seh spehtseeyahlno oboochehm zahr neh
Thank you very much for an enjoyable evening.	**Hvala Vam, bilo je prijatno veče.**	hvahlah vahm beelo yeh preeyahtno vehcheh
I'm afraid we've got to go now.	**Nažalost sad moramo da idemo.**	nahzhahlost sahd morahmo dah eedehmo
Next time you must come to us.	**Sledeći put Vi morate doći kod nas.**	slehdehcheh poot vee morahteh dochee kod nahs
Thanks for the party. It was great.	**Hvala Vam na društvu. Bilo je divno.**	hvahlah vahm nah drooshtvoo. beelo yeh deevno

* Feminine. See grammar.

The weather

They talk about the weather just as much in Yugoslavia as the British are supposed to do. So...

What a lovely day!	**Kakav divan dan!**	kahkahv deevahn dahn
What awful weather for this time of year!	**Kakvo strašno vreme za ovo doba godine!**	kahkvo strahshno vrehmeh zah ovo dobah godeeneh
Isn't it cold today?	**Danas je hladno, zar ne?**	dahnahs yeh hlahdno zahr neh
Isn't it hot today?	**Danas je toplo, zar ne?**	dahnahs yeh toplo zahr neh
Is it usually as warm as this?	**Da li je obično ovako toplo kao danas?**	dah lee yeh obeechno ovahko toplo kaho dahnahs
It's very foggy, isn't it?	**Vrlo je maglovito, zar ne?**	verlo yeh mahgloveeto zahr neh
What's the temperature outside?	**Kakva je temperatura napolju?**	kahkvah yeh tehmpehrahtoorah nahpol'oo

Dating

Would you like a cigarette?	**Želite li cigaretu?**	zhehleeteh lee tseegahrehtoo
Have you got a light, please?	**Imate li šibice?**	eemahteh lee sheebeetseh
Can I get you a drink?	**Da li bih Vam mogao doneti neko piće?**	dah lee beeh vahm mogaho donehtee nehko peecheh
Excuse me, could you help me?	**Izvinite, da li biste mi mogli pomoći?**	eezveeneeteh dah lee beesteh mee moglee pomochee
I'm lost. Can you show me the way to...?	**Zalutao sam. Možete li mi poka- zati put za...?**	zahlootaho sahm. mozhehteh mee pokahzahtee poot zah
Are you waiting for someone?	**Da li čekate nekoga?**	dah lee chehkahteh nehkogah

MAKING FRIENDS

Are you free this evening?	Da li ste slobodni večeras?	dah lee steh slobodnee vehchehrahs
Would you like to come out with me tonight?	Da li biste hteli da izadjete sa mnom večeras?	dah lee beesteh htehlee dah eezahjehteh sah mnom vehchehrahs
Would you like to go dancing?	Da li biste išli na ples?	dah lee beesteh eeshlee nah plehs
I know a good discotheque.	Znam jednu dobru diskoteku.	znahm yehdnoo dobroo deeskotehkoo
Shall we go to the cinema (movies)?	Mogli bismo ići u kino.	moglee beesmo eechee oo keeno
Would you like to go for a drive?	Da li biste hteli da se provozamo kolima?	dah lee beesteh htehlee dah seh provozahmo koleemah
I'd love to, thank you.	Hvala lepo, volela bih (voleo bih*).	hvahlah lehpo volehlah beeh (voleho beeh)
Where shall we meet?	Gde ćemo se naći?	gdeh chehmo seh nahchee
What time shall I meet you?	Kad ću Vas videti?	kahd choo vahs veedehtee
I'll pick you up at the hotel.	Doći ću po Vas u hotel.	dochee choo po vahs oo hotehl
I'll call for you at eight.	Doći ću po Vas u osam sati.	dochee choo po vahs oo osahm sahtee
May I take you home?	Mogu li Vas otpratiti kući?	mogoo lee vahs otprahteetee koochee
Can I see you again tomorrow?	Mogu li Vas videti sutra opet?	mogoo lee vahs veedehtee sootrah opeht
Thank you, it's been a wonderful evening.	Hvala Vam, bilo je divno veče.	hvahlah vahm beelo yeh deevno vehcheh
Thanks, it was a fabulous time.	Hvala, bilo je krasno.	hvahlah beelo yeh krahsno
What's your telephone number?	Koji je Vaš telefonski broj?	koyee yeh vahsh tehlehfonskee broy
Do you have your own apartment?	Da li imate svoj stan?	dah lee eemahteh svoy stahn
Do you live alone?	Da li živite sami?	dah lee zheeveeteh sahmee
What time is your last train?	Kad ide Vaš poslednji voz [vlak]?	kahd eedeh vahsh poslehdñeh voz [vlahk]

* Masculine. See grammar.

Shopping guide

This shopping guide is designed to help you find what you want with ease, accuracy and speed. It features:

1. a list of all major shops, stores and services;

2. some general expressions required when shopping to allow you to be specific and selective;

3. full details of the shops and services most likely to concern you. Here you'll find advice, alphabetical lists of items and conversion charts listed under the headings below.

	Main items	Page
Bookshop	books, magazines, newspapers, stationery	104
Camping	camping equipment	106
Chemist's (Pharmacy)	medicine, first-aid, cosmetics, toiletry	108
Clothing	clothes, shoes	112
Electrical appliances	radios, tape-recorders, etc., and records	119
Hairdresser's	barber's, ladies' hairdresser's, beauty parlour	121
Jeweller's	jewellery, watches	123
Laundry/ dry cleaning	usual facilities	126
Photography	cameras, films, developing	127
Provisions	this is confined to basic items required for picnics	129
Souvenirs	souvenirs and gifts to take home	131
Tobacconist's	smokers' requisites	132

SHOPPING GUIDE

Advice

If you have a pretty clear idea of what you want before you set
out, do a little homework first. Look under the appropriate
heading, pick out the article and find a suitable description for
it (colour, material, etc.). If you just happen to wander into a
shop, turn to the appropriate heading and tackle the conversation step by step, as shown.

Shops in Yugoslavia usually open around 8 a.m., some at 9.
They close at 7 or 8 p.m. Some close for lunch at noon and open
at 4 p.m. A lot of shops are open non-stop from 8 a.m. to 8 p.m.
Some food shops are open on Sundays from 7 a.m. until 10 a.m.
All shops are open on Saturdays until 3 p.m. and some even
until 8 p.m.

Shops, stores and services

Where's the nearest... ?	**Gde je najbliža... ?**	gdeh yeh **nahy**bleezhah
antique shop	**radnja sa starinama**	**rahd**ñah sah stah**ree**nahmah
art gallery	**umetnička galerija**	oomeht**neech**kah gah**leh**reeyah
baker's	**pekara**	**peh**kahrah
bank	**banka**	**bahn**kah
barber's	**berberin**	**behr**behreen
beauty parlour	**kozmetički salon**	kozmeh**teech**kee **sah**lon
bookshop	**knjižara**	**kñee**zhahrah
butcher's	**mesarnica**	**meh**sahrneetsah
cable office	**pošta**	**posh**tah
camera store	**radnja sa foto materijalom**	**rahd**ñah sah foto **mah**teh-reeyahlom
candy store	**radnja sa slatkišima**	**rahd**ñah sah slaht**kee**sheemah
chemist's	**drogerija**	droge**hreh**yah
cigar store	**trafika**	trah**fee**kah
confectionery	**poslastičarnica**	poslah**stee**chahrneetsah
dairy	**mlečni restoran [mlekara]**	**mlehch**nee reh**sto**rahn [**mleh**kahrah]
delicatessen	**delikatesna radnja**	dehleekah**tehs**nah **rahd**ñah
dentist	**zubni lekar**	**zoob**nee **leh**kahr
department store	**robna kuća**	**rob**nah **koo**chah
doctor	**lekar/doktor**	**leh**kahr/**dok**tor
dressmaker's	**krojačica**	kroyah**cheet**sah
dry cleaner's	**hemijska čistiona**	**heh**meeyskah cheestee**o**nah

filling station	**benzinska stanica**	**behn**zeenskah **stah**neetsah
fishmonger	**radnja sa ribom** [ribarnica]	rahd**ñah sah reebom** [**reeb**ahrneetsah]
florist's	**cvećarnica**	**tsveh**chahrneetsah
furrier's	**krznar**	**kerz**nahr
garage	**garaža**	gah**rah**zhah
greengrocer's	**piljarnica**	**peel**[v]ahrneetsah
hairdresser's (ladies)	**frizer**	**free**zehr
hardware store	**gvožđarska radnja**	**gvozh**jahrskah **rahd**ñah
hat shop	**radnja sa šeširima**	rahd**ñah sah shehsheer**eemah
hospital	**bolnica**	**bol**neetsah
launderette (laundromat)	**automatska perionica veša**	ahooto**maht**skah pehree**oo**neetsa **veh**shah
laundry	**vešernica**	**veh**shehrneetsah
liquor store (off-licence)	**radnja sa alkoholnim pićem**	rahd**ñah sah ahl**koholneem **pee**chehm
milliner's	**modiskinja**	modees**kee**ñah
newsstand	**kiosk sa novinama**	**kee**osk sah no**veen**ahmah
optician	**optičar**	**opt**eechahr
pastry shop	**poslastičarnica**	poslah**steec**hahrneetsah
pawnbroker's	**zalagaonica**	zahlahgaho**neet**sah
pharmacy	**apoteka**	ahpo**teh**kah
photographer's (studio)	**fotograf**	foto**grahf**
photo store	**radnja sa foto materijalom**	rahd**ñah sah foto mahtehreey**ahlom
police station	**milicijska stanica**	mee**leet**seeyskah **stah**neetsah
post office	**pošta**	**posh**tah
shoemaker's (repairs)	**obućar** [postolar]	oboo**chahr** [posto**lahr**]
shoe shop	**prodavnica cipela**	prodahv**neetsah tsee**pehlah
souvenir shop	**prodavnica suvenira**	prodahv**neetsah** soovehn**eer**ah
sporting goods store	**prodavnica sportske opreme**	prodahv**neetsah sportskeh** op**reh**meh
stationer's	**papirnica**	pah**peer**neetsah
supermarket	**samoposluga**	sahmoposl**oog**ah
tailor's	**krojač**	**kroy**ahch
tobacconist's	**trafika**	**trahf**eekah
toy shop	**radnja sa igračkama**	rahd**ñah sah eegrahch**kahmah
travel agent	**turistička agencija**	toor**eest**eechkah ah**gehnt**seeyah
watchmaker's	**časovničar** [urar]	**chah**sovneechahr [**oor**ahr]
wine merchant's	**prodavnica vina**	prodahv**neetsah veen**ah

SHOPPING GUIDE

RASPRODAJA	SALE

General expressions

Here are some expressions which will be useful to you when you're out shopping:

Where?

Where's the nearest...?	**Gde je najbliži...?**	gdeh yeh **nahy**bleezhee
Where's a good...?	**Gde je dobar/ dobra...?**	gdeh yeh **do**bahr/**do**brah
Where can I get...?	**Gde mogu da dobijem...?**	gdeh **mo**goo dah **do**beeyehm
Can you recommend an inexpensive...?	**Možete li mi preporučiti jeftin...**	**mo**zhehteh lee mee prehporoo**chee**teh **yehf**teen
Where's the main shopping area?	**Gde je glavni trgovački centar?**	gdeh yeh **glahv**nee **ter**go-vahchkee **tsehn**tahr
How far is it from here?	**Koliko je daleko odavde?**	**ko**leeko yeh **dah**lehko o**dahv**deh
How do I get there?	**Kako mogu da dodjem tamo?**	**kah**ko **mo**goo dah **do**dyehm **tah**mo

Service

Can you help me?	**Možete li mi pomoći?**	**mo**zhehteh lee mee **po**mochee
I'm just looking around.	**Samo razgledam.**	**sah**mo rahz**gleh**dahm
I'd like...	**Želim...**	**zheh**leem
Have you any...?	**Imate li...?**	**ee**mahteh lee

That one

Can you show me...?	**Možete li mi pokazati...?**	**mo**zhehteh lee mee po**kah**zahtee
that/those	**onaj/one**	**o**nahy/**o**neh
the one in the window	**onaj u izlogu**	**o**nahy oo **eez**logoo
It's over there.	**Tamo preko se nalazi.**	**tah**mo **preh**ko seh **nah**lahzee

Defining the article

I'd like a...one.	**Želim jedan/jednu/ jedno...**	zhehleem yehdahn/yehdnoo yehdno
big	**veliki**	vehleekee
cheap	**jeftini**	yehfteenee
dark	**tamni**	tahmnee
good	**dobar**	dobahr
heavy	**teški**	tehshkee
large	**veliki**	vehleekee
light (weight)	**lagani**	lahgahnee
light (colour)	**svetli**	svehtlee
oval	**ovalni**	ovahlnee
rectangular	**pravougaoni**	prahvooogahonee
round	**okrugli**	okrooglee
small	**mali**	mahlee
square	**četvrtasti**	chehtvertahstee
I don't want anything too expensive.	**Ne želim ništa suviše skupo.**	neh zhehleem neeshtah sooveesheh skoopo

Preference

I prefer something of better quality.	**Više bih voleo (volela*) nešto boljeg kvaliteta.**	veesheh beeh voleho (volehlah) nehshto bolʸehg kvahleetehtah
Can you show me some more?	**Možete li mi pokazati još nešto?**	mozhehteh lee mee pokahzahtee yosh nehshto
Haven't you anything...?	**Imate li nešto...?**	eemahteh lee nehshto
cheaper/better	**jeftinije/bolje**	yehfteeneeyeh/bolʸeh
larger/smaller	**veće/manje**	vehcheh/mahñeh

How much?

How much is this?	**Koliko košta ovo?**	koleeko koshtah ovo
I don't understand. Please write it down.	**Ja ne razumem. Molim Vas napišite mi to.**	yah neh rahzoomehm. moleem vahs nahpeesheetee mee to
I don't want to spend more than...	**Ne želim potrošiti više od...**	neh zhehleem potrosheetee veesheh od

* Feminine. See grammar.

FOR COLOURS, see page 112

SHOPPING GUIDE

Decision

That's just what I want.	**To je baš što mi treba.**	to yeh bahsh shto mee **treh**bah
No, I don't like it.	**Ne, ne dopada mi se.**	neh neh **do**pahdah mee seh
I'll take it.	**Uzeću ovo.**	**oo**zehchoo ovo

Ordering

Can you order it for me?	**Možete li mi ovo poručiti?**	**mo**zhehteh lee mee ovo poroo**chee**teetee
How long will it take?	**Koliko dugo će trebati?**	ko**lee**ko **doo**go cheh **treh**bahtee
I'd like it as soon as possible.	**Želeo (Želela*) bih to što pre.**	**zheh**leho (**zheh**lehlah) beeh to shto preh

Delivery

I'll take it with me.	**Poneću sa sobom.**	**po**nehchoo sah **so**bom
Deliver it to the... hotel.	**Pošaljite to u... hotel.**	poshahl'eeteh to oo...**ho**tehl
Please send it to this address.	**Pošaljite molim Vas na ovu adresu.**	poshahl'eeteh **mo**leem vahs nah **o**voo ah**dreh**soo
Will I have any difficulty with the customs?	**Da li ću imati teškoća na carini?**	dah lee choo **ee**mahtee teh**shko**chah nah **tsah**reenee

Paying

How much is it?	**Koliko košta?**	ko**lee**ko **kosh**tah
Can I pay by traveller's cheque?	**Mogu li da platim putnim čekovima?**	**mo**goo lee dah **plah**teem **poot**neem **cheh**koveemah
Do you accept credit cards?	**Da li primate kreditne karte?**	dah lee **pree**mahteh **kreh**deetneh **kahr**teh
Haven't you made a mistake in the bill?	**Da niste progrešili u računu?**	dah **nees**teh pogreh**shee**lee oo rah**choo**noo
Can I have a receipt, please?	**Mogu li da dobijem račun, molim Vas?**	**mo**goo lee dah **do**beeyehm **rah**choon **mo**leem vahs
Will you wrap it, please?	**Hoćete li mi ovo upakovati?**	**ho**chehteh lee mee ovo oopahko**vah**tee
Have you got a carrier bag?	**Imate li kesu za nošenje?**	**ee**mahteh lee **keh**soo zah **no**shehñeh

* Feminine. See Grammar.

Anything else?

No, thanks, that's all.	Ne hvala to je sve.	neh hvahlah to yeh sveh
Yes, I want.../ Show me...	Da. Želim.../ Pokažite mi...	dah zhehleem.../ pokahzheeteh mee
Thank you. Good-bye.	Hvala. Dovidjenja.	hvahlah. doveejehñah

Dissatisfied

Can you change this, please?	Možete li mi ovo zameniti, molim Vas?	mozhehteh lee mee ovo zahmehneetee moleem vahs
I want to return this.	Želim ovo da vratim.	zhehleem ovo dah vrahteem
I'd like a refund. Here's the receipt.	Želeo bih da mi vratite novac. Ovo je moj račun.	zhehleho beeh dah mee vrahteeteh novahts. ovo yeh moy rahchoon

SHOPPING GUIDE

Possible answers

Mogu li Vam pomoći?	Can I help you?
Šta želite?	What would you like?
Koju...bi željeli?	What...would you like?
boju/oblik kvalitet/količinu	colour/shape quality/quantity
Žao mi je, nemamo više.	I'm sorry, we haven't any.
Nemamo više u zalihi.	We're out of stock.
Hoćete li da poručimo za Vas?	Shall we order it for you?
Hoćete li ih poneti ili hoćete da ih pošaljemo?	Will you take it with you or shall we send it?
To je..., molim.	That's..., please.
Kasa je tamo.	The cashier is over there.
Ne primamo...	We don't accept...
kreditne karte putne čekove lične čekove	credit cards traveller's cheques personal cheques

Bookshop – Stationer's – Newsstand

Bookshops and stationers are generally separate shops in Yugoslavia, although some bookshops may sell magazines and foreign newspapers in particular. Kiosks are found everywhere.

Where's the nearest...?	**Gde je najbliža...?**	gdeh yeh **nah**ybleezhah
bookshop	**knjižara**	kñeezhahrah
stationer's	**papirnica**	pahpeerneetsah
newsstand	**kiosk s novinama**	keeosk s noveenahmah
Can you recommend a good bookshop?	**Možete li mi preporučiti dobru knjižaru?**	mozhehteh lee mee prehporoocheetee dobroo kñeezhahroo
Where can I buy an English newspaper?	**Gde mogu kupiti engleske novine?**	gdeh mogoo koopeetee ehnglehskeh noveeneh
I want to buy a/an/some...	**Želim da kupim...**	zhehleem da koopeem
address book	**adresar**	ahdrehsahr
ball-point pen	**hemijsku olovku**	hehmeeyskoo olovkoo
book	**knjigu**	kñeegoo
box of paints	**kutiju boja**	kooteeyoo boyah
carbon paper	**indigo**	eendeego
crayons	**bojice**	boyeetseh
dictionary	**rečnik**	rehchneek
English-Serbo-Croatian	**englesko-srpskohrvatski**	ehnglehskoo serpskohervahtskee
Serbo-Croatian-English	**srpskohrvatsko-engleski**	serpskohervahtskoo ehnglehskee
pocket dictionary	**džepni rečnik**	jehpnee rehchneek
drawing paper	**papir za crtanje**	pahpeer zah tsertahneh
drawing pins	**rajsnegle**	rahysnehgleh
envelopes	**koverte**	kovehrteh
eraser	**gumu za brisanje**	goomoo zah breesahñeh
exercise book	**svesku [teku]**	svehskoo [tehkoo]
file	**fascikl**	fahstseekl
fountain pen	**naliv pero**	nahleev pehro
glue	**lepilo**	lehpeelo
grammar book	**gramatiku**	grahmahteekoo
guide book	**vodič**	vodeech
ink	**mastilo [tintu]**	mahsteelo [teentoo]
black/red/blue	**crno/crveno/plavo**	tserno/tservehno/plahvo

magazine	časopis	chahsopees
map	geografsku kartu	gehografhskoo kahrtoo
map of the town	kartu grada	kahrtoo grahdah
road map	kartu puteva	kahrtoo pootehvah
newspaper	novine	noveeneh
American/English	američke/ engleske	ahmehreechkeh/ ehnglehskeh
notebook	beležnicu [blok]	behlehzhneetsoo [blok]
paperback	džepnu knjigu	jehpnoo kñeegoo
paper napkins	salvete od hartije	sahlvehteh od hahrteeyeh
paste	lepak	lehpahk
pen	pero	pehro
pencil	olovku	olovkoo
pencil sharpener	oštrač za olovke	oshtrahch zah olovkeh
playing cards	karte za igranje	kahrteh zah eegrahñeh
postcards	dopisnice	dopeesneetseh
rubber bands	gumice	goomeetseh
ruler	lenjir	lehñeer
sketching block	skicenblok	skeetsehnblok
string	kanap	kahnahpah
thumb tacks	rajsnegle	rahysnehgleh
tissue paper	tanki papir	tahnkee pahpeer
tracing paper	paus papir	pahoos pahpeer
typewriter ribbon	vrpcu za mašinu	verptsoo zah mahsheenoo
typing paper	papir za mašinu	pahpeer zah mahsheenoo
wrapping paper	pakpapir	pahkpahpeerah
writing pad	blok za pisanje	blok zah peesahneh
Where's the guide-book section?	Gde je odelenje sa turističkim vodičima?	gdeh yeh odehlehneh sah tooreesteechkeem vodeecheemah
Where do you keep the English books?	Gde držite engleske knjige?	gdeh derzheeteh ehnglehskeh kñeegeh

SHOPPING GUIDE

Here are some modern authors whose books are available in English translation:

Ivo Andrić	Miroslav Krleža
Miodrag Bulatović	Gordana Olujić
Dobrica Ćosić	Meša Selimović

Camping

Here we are concerned with the equipment you may need.

I'd like a/an/some…	Želeo bih…	zhehleho beeh
axe	**sekiru**	**seh**keeroo
bottle opener	**otvarač za flaše**	otva**h**rahch zah flahsheh
bucket	**kantu**	**kah**ntoo
butane gas	**butan gas**	**boo**tahn gahs
camp bed	**poljski krevet**	pol^yskee **kreh**veht
camping equipment	**opremu za**	**o**prehmoo zah
	kampovanje	**kahm**povahñeh
can opener	**otvarač za konzerve**	otva**h**rahch zah **kon**zehrveh
candles	**sveće**	**sveh**cheh
chair	**stolicu**	**sto**leetsoo
folding chair	**stolicu za**	**sto**leetsoo zah
	sklapanje	**sklah**pahñeh
compass	**kompas**	**kom**pahs
corkscrew	**vadičep**	**vah**deechehp
crockery	**zemljano sudje**	zehml^yahno soojeh
cutlery	**jedaći pribor**	**yeh**dahchee **pree**bor
deck chair	**ligeštul**	**lee**gehshtool
first-aid kit	**opremu za prvu**	**o**prehmoo zah **per**voo
	pomoć	**po**moch
fishing tackle	**pribor za pecanje**	**pree**bor zah **peh**tsahñeh
flashlight	**baterijsku lampu**	bah**teh**reeyskoo **lahm**poo
frying pan	**tiganj**	**tee**gahñ
groundsheet	**platno za zemlju**	**plaht**no zah **zehm**l^yoo
hammer	**čekić**	**cheh**keech
hammock	**mrežu za ležanje**	**mrehz**hoo zah **lehz**hahñeh
ice-bag	**frižider za kola**	**freezhee**dehr zah **ko**lah
kerosine	**petrolej za**	**pehtro**lehy zah **sveh**teel^ykeh
	svetiljke	
kettle	**kotlić**	**kot**leech
knapsack	**ranac**	**rah**nahts
lamp	**lampu**	**lahm**poo
lantern	**fenjer**	**feh**ñehr
matches	**šibice**	**shee**beetseh
mattress	**madrac**	**mah**drahts
methylated spirits	**špiritus**	**shpee**reetoos
mosquito net	**mrežu protiv**	**mrehz**hoo **pro**teev
	komaraca	**komah**rahtsah
pail	**kofu**	**ko**foo
paraffin	**petrolej za svetiljke**	**pehtro**lehy zah **sveh**teel^ykeh
penknife	**džepni nožić**	**jehp**nee **no**zheech

picnic case	**torbu za piknik**	tor**boo** zah **peek**neek
pressure cooker	**ekspres lonac na paru**	**ehks**prehs **lo**nahts nah **pah**roo
primus stove	**primus**	**pree**moos
rope	**konopac**	**ko**nopahts
rucksack	**ruksak**	**roo**ksahk
saucepan	**šerpu**	**shehr**poo
scissors	**makaze**	**mah**kahzeh
screwdriver	**šrafciger**	**shrahf**tseegehr
sleeping bag	**vreću za spavanje**	**vreh**choo zah **spah**vahñeh
stewpan	**tiganj**	**tee**gahñ
stove	**štednjak**	**shtehd**ñahk
table	**sto**	sto
folding table	**sto za sklapanje**	sto zah **sklah**pahñeh
tent	**šator**	**shah**tor
tent peg	**kuku za šator**	**koo**koo zah **shah**tor
tent pole	**motku za šator**	**mot**koo zah **shah**tor
thermos flask (bottle)	**termos flašu**	**teh**rmos **flah**shoo
tin opener	**otvarač za konzerve**	**ot**vahrahch zah **kon**zehrveh
torch	**baterijsku lampu**	**bah**tehreeyskoo **lah**mpoo
vacuum flask	**termos**	**teh**rmos
water carrier	**putnu flašu za vodu**	**poot**noo **flah**shoo zah **vo**doo
wood alcohol	**špiritus**	**shpee**reetoos

SHOPPING GUIDE

Crockery
cups	**šoljice**	**shol**ʸeetseh
food box	**kutija za hranu**	**koo**teeyah zah **hrah**noo
mugs	**vrčevi**	**ver**chehvee
plates	**tanjiri**	**tah**ñeeree
saucers	**tanjirići**	**tah**ñeereechee

Cutlery
forks	**viljuške**	**veel**ʸooshkeh
knives	**noževi**	**no**zhehvee
dessert knife	**mali noževi**	**mah**lee **no**zhehvee
spoons	**kašike**	**kah**sheekeh
teaspoons	**male kašike**	**mah**leh **kah**sheekeh
(made of) plastic	**(od) plastike**	(od) **plah**steekeh
(made of) stainless steel	**(od) nerdjajućeg čelika**	(od) **neh**rjahyoochehg **cheh**leekah

Chemist's (pharmacy) – Drugstore

There is a marked distinction in Yugoslavia between an *apoteka* (ahpo**teh**kah) and a *drogerija* (dro**geh**reeyah). In an *apoteka* you'll find both non-prescription medicines and those made up according to a prescription. In a *drogerija* you'll find a great range of toilet articles, cosmetics and the like; sometimes films, too. However, you'll find *drogerija* in large cities only.

In the window of an *apoteka* you'll see a notice telling you where the nearest all-night chemist is. In larger cities, some chemists are open day and night. Their names and addresses can be found in daily newspapers.

For ease of reading, this section has been divided into two parts:

1. Pharmaceutical – medicine, first-aid, etc.
2. Toiletry – toilet articles, cosmetics.

General

Where's the nearest (all-night) chemist?	**Gde je najbliža (dežurna) apoteka?**	gdeh yeh **nahy**bleezhah (**dehzh**oornah) ahpo**teh**kah
What time does the chemist open?	**Kad se apoteka otvara?**	kahd seh ahpo**teh**kah otvahrah
When does the chemist close?	**Kad se apoteka zatvara?**	kahd seh ahpo**teh**kah **zah**tvahrah

Part 1 – Pharmaceutical

I want something for...	**Trebam nešto protiv...**	**treh**bahm **neh**shto **pro**teev
a cold/a cough	**prehlade/kašlja**	**preh**hlahdeh/**kah**shl^yah
hay fever	**polenske groznice**	**po**lehnskeh **groz**neetseh
a hangover	**mamurluka**	mahmoor**loo**kah
sunburn	**opekotina od sunca**	ope**hko**teenah od **soon**tsah
travel sickness	**putne bolesti**	**poot**neh bo**leh**stee
Can you make me up this prescription?	**Možete li mi napraviti lek po ovom receptu?**	**mo**zhehteh lee mee nah**prah**veeteh lahk po ovom reht**sehp**too
Shall I wait?	**Treba li da pričekam?**	**treh**bah lee dah **pree**chehkahm

FOR DOCTOR, see page 162

When shall I come back?	Kad se mogu vratiti?	kahd seh mogoo vrahteetee
Can I get it without a prescription?	Da li ga mogu dobiti bez recepta?	dah lee gah mogoo dobeetee behz rehtsehptah
Can I have a/an/some...?	Mogu li da dobijem...?	mogoo lee dah dobeeyehm
antiseptic cream	antiseptičnu mast	ahnteesehpteechnoo mahst
bandage	zavoj	zahvoy
calcium tablets	kalcijum tablete	kahltseeyoom tahblehteh
castor oil	ricinusovo ulje	reetseenoosovo oolʸeh
contraceptives	kontraceptivno sredstvo	kontrahahtsehpteevno srehdstvo
corn pads	flaster za žuljeve	flahstehr zah zhoolʸehveh
cotton wool	vatu	vahtoo
cough lozenges	tablete za kašalj	tahblehteh zah kahshahlʸ
diabetic lozenges	pastile za dijabetičare	pahsteeleh zah deeyahbehteechahreh
disinfectant	dezinfekciono sredstvo	dehzeenfehktseeono srehdstvo
ear drops	kapi za uvo	kahpee zah oovo
elastoplast (band-aid)	hanzaplast	hahnzahplahst
eye drops	kapi za oči	kahpee zah ochee
gargle (mouthwash)	sredstvo za ispiranje usta	srehdstvo zah eespeerahñeh oostah
gauze	gazu	gahzoo
gauze bandage	zavoj sa gazom	zahvoy sah gahzom
insect repellant	sredstvo protiv insekata	srehdstvo proteev eensehkahtah
iodine	jod	yod
iron pills/tablets	pilule/tablete gvožđa	peelooleh/tahblehteh gvozhjah
laxative	laksativ	lahksahteev
sanitary napkins	mesečne uloške	mehsehchneh ooloshkeh
sleeping pills	pilule za spavanje	peelooleh zah spahvahñeh
stomach pills	pilule za stomak	peelooleh zah stomahk
tissues	papirne maramice	pahpeerneh mahrahmeetseh
throat lozenges	pilule za grlo	peelooleh zah gerlo
tranquillizers	sredstva za umirenje	srehdstvah zah oomeerehñeh
vitamin pills	vitamin-tablete	veetahmeen tahblehteh

SHOPPING GUIDE

| OTROV! | POISON! |
| SAMO ZA SPOLJNU UPOTREBU | FOR EXTERNAL USE ONLY |

Part 2 – Toiletry

Can I have a/an/some...?	Mogu li da dobijem...?	mogoo lee dah dobeeyehm
acne cream	mast za akne	mahst zah ahkneh
after-shave lotion	after šeiv losion	ahftehr sheheev loseeon ...
astringent	stipsu	steepsoo
bath salts	so za kupanje	so zah koopahñeh
cream	kremu	krehmoo
cleansing cream	kremu za čišćenje lica	krehmoo zah cheeshchehñeh leetsah
cold cream	hladnu kremu	hlahdnoo krehmoo
enzyme cream	enzim kremu	ehnzeem krehmoo
foundation cream	podlogu za šminku	podlogoo zah shmeenkoo
hormone cream	hormonalnu kremu	hormonahlnoo krehmoo
moisturizing cream	vlažnu kremu	vlahzhnoo krehmoo
night cream	kremu za noć	krehmoo zah noch
cuticle remover	sredstvo za otklanjanje zanoktica	srehdstvo zah otklahñahñeh zahnokteetsah
deodorant (spray)	deodorant (sprei)	dehodorahnt (sprehee)
eau de Cologne	kolonjsku vodu	koloñskoo vodoo
emery board	šmirgl papir	shmeergl pahpeer
eye liner	lajner za oči	lahynehr zah ochee
eye pencil	krejon za oči	krehyon zah ochee
eye shadow	senku za oči	sehnkoo zah ochee
face pack	antirid masku	ahnteereed mahskoo
face powder	puder za lice	poodehr zah leetseh
foot cream	kremu za stopala	krehmoo zah stopahlah
hand cream	kremu za ruke	krehmoo zah rookeh
lipsalve	pomadu za usne	pomahdoo zah oosneh
lipstick	ruž za usne	roozh zah oosneh
lipstick brush	četku za ruž	chehtkoo zah roozh
make-up bag	kutiju za kozmetiku	kooteeyoo zah kozmehteekoo
make-up remover pads	tampone za brisanje lica	tahmponeh zah breesahñeh leetsah
nail brush	četku za nokte	chehtkoo zah nokteh
nail file	turpiju za nokte	toorpeeyoo zah nokteh
nail lacquer	lak	lahk
nail lacquer remover	aceton	ahtsehton
nail scissors	makaze za nokte	mahkahzeh zah nokteh
perfume	parfem	pahrfehm
cream/spray	krem/sprei	krehm/sprehee
powder puff	pufnu za puder	poofnoo zah poodehr
razor	aparat za brijanje	ahpahraht zah breeyahñeh
razor blades	žilete	zheelehteh
rouge (cream/powder)	ruž (krem/puder)	roozh (krehm/poodehr)

safety pins	zihernadle	zeehehrnahdleh
shampoo	šampon	shampon
shaving brush	četku za brijanje	chehtkoo zah breeyahñeh
shaving cream (brushless)	kremu za brijanje (bez četke)	krehmoo zah breeyahñeh (behz chehtkeh)
shaving soap	sapun za brijanje	sahpoon zah breeyahñeh
soap	sapun	sahpoon
sponge	sundjer [spužva]	soonjehr [spoozhvah]
sun-tan cream/oil	kremu/ulje za sunčanje	krehmoo/oolyeh zah soonchahñe
talcum powder	talk	tahlk
toilet bag	torbicu za šminku	torbeetsoo zah shmeenkoo
tooth brush	četkicu za zube	chehtkeetsoo zah zoobeh
toothpaste	pastu za zube	pahstoo zah zoobeh
wash-off face cleanser	sredstvo za čišćenje lica	srehdstvo zah cheeshchehñeh leetsah

For your hair

brush	četku [kefu]	chehtkoo [kehfoo]
colourant	preliv	prehleev
comb	češalj	chehshahlʸ
cream	kremu za kosu	krehmoo zah kosoo
dye	boju za kosu	boyoo zah kosoo
grips (bobby pins)	šnale	shnahleh
oil	ulje za kosu	oolʸeh zah kosoo
lacquer (spray)	lak za kosu	lahk zah kosoo
piece	šinjon	sheeñon
pins	šnale	shnahleh
rollers	viklere	veeklehreh
setting lotion	lak za kosu	lahk zah kosoo

For the baby

beaker	bokal	bokahl
bibs	portiklu	porteekloo
cream	kremu	krehmoo
food	hranu	hrahnoo
nappies (diapers)	pelene	pehlehneh
nappy pins	pribadače za pelenu	preebahdahcheh zah pehlehnoo
oil	ulje	oolʸeh
oil sheet	gumeni podmetač	goomehnee podmehtahch
powder	puder	poodehr
rubber pants	gumene gaćice	goomehneh gahcheetseh

Clothing

If you want to buy something specific, prepare yourself in advance. Look at the list of clothing on page 117. Get some idea of the colour, material and size you want. They're all listed in the next few pages.

General

I'd like...	**Želim...**	zhehleem
I want...for a 10-year-old boy.	**Želim...za 10 godišnjeg dečka.**	zhehleem...zah 10 godeeshñehg **deh**chkah
I want something like this.	**Želim nešto slično ovom.**	zhehleem **neh**shto **sleech**no **ov**om
I like the one in the window.	**Želim onaj u izlogu.**	zhehleem onahy oo eezlogoo
How much is that per metre?	**Koliko košta jedan metar?**	ko**lee**ko koshtah yehdahn **meh**tahr

1 centimetre = 0.39 in.	1 inch = 2.54 cm.
1 metre = 39.37 in.	1 foot = 30.5 cm.
10 metres = 32.81 ft.	1 yard = 0.91 m.

Colour

I want something in...	**Želim nešto u...**	zhehleem **neh**shto oo
I want a darker shade.	**Želim tamnije.**	zhehleem tahm**nee**eyeh
I want something to match this.	**Želim nešto što se slaže s ovim.**	zhehleem **neh**shto shto seh **slah**zheh s oveem
I don't like the colour.	**Ne svidja mi se boja.**	neh **svee**jah mee seh **bo**yah

beige	**bež**	behzh
black	**crno**	tserno
blue	**plavo**	plahvo
brown	**braon**	brahon
cream	**krem**	krehm
crimson	**grimizno**	greemeezno
emerald	**smaragdno zeleno**	smahrahgdno zehlehno
fawn	**svetlo braon**	svehtlo brahon
gold	**boja zlata**	boyah zlahtah
green	**zeleno**	zehlehno
grey	**sivo**	seevo
mauve	**lila**	leelah
orange	**oranž**	orahnzh
pink	**roza**	rozah
red	**crveno**	tservehno
scarlet	**tamno crveno**	tahmno tservehno
silver	**srebreno**	srehbrehno
tan	**braonkasto**	brahonkahsto
white	**belo**	behlo
yellow	**žuto**	zhooto

štrafasto
(**shtrah**fahsto)

na tačkice
(nah **tahch**keetseh)

karo
(**kah**ro)

dezenirano
(dehzehneerahno)

Material

Have you anything in...?	**Imate li nešto u...?**	eemahteh lee nehshto oo
Is that made here?	**Da li se to pravi ovde?**	dah lee seh to prahvee ovdeh
hand-made	**ručna izrada**	roochnah eezrahdah
ready-made	**gotovo [konfekcija]**	gotovo [konfehktseeyah]
custom-made	**po meri**	po mehree
Have you any better quality?	**Imate li bolji kvalitet?**	eemahteh lee bolʹee kvahleeteht
I want something thinner.	**Želeo bih nešto tanje.**	zhehleho beeh nehshto tahñeh

What's it made of?	**Od čega je to?**	od **cheh**gah yeh to

It may be made of...

cambric	**batist**	bah**teest**
camel-hair	**kamelher**	**kah**mehlhehr
chiffon	**šifon**	**shee**fon
corduroy	**rebrasti somot**	**reh**brahstee somot
cotton	**pamuk**	**pah**mook
felt	**filc**	**feelts**
flannel	**flanel**	**flah**nehl
lace	**čipka**	**cheep**kah
leather	**koža**	**ko**zhah
linen	**platno**	**plah**tno
nylon	**najlon**	**nah**ylon
piqué	**pike**	**pee**keh
rayon	**rejon**	**reh**yon
rubber	**guma**	**goo**mah
satin	**saten**	**sah**tehn
silk	**svila**	**svee**lah
suede	**jelenja koža**	**yeh**lehñah **ko**zhah
towelling	**frotir**	**fro**teer
tulle	**til**	**teel**
tweed	**twid**	**tveed**
velvet	**somot**	**so**mot
wool	**vuna**	**voo**nah
synthetic	**sintetika**	seen**teh**teekah
drip-dry (non-iron)	**što se ne pegla**	shto sen neh **pehg**lah
crease-resistant	**što se ne gužva**	shto seh neh **goozh**vah

Size

My size is 38.	**Moja mera je 38.**	**moy**ah **meh**rah yeh 38
Our sizes are different at home. Could you measure me?	**Kod nas su brojevi drukčiji. Možete li me izmeriti?**	kod nahs soo **bro**yehvee **drook**cheeyee. **mozh**ehteh lee meh **eez**mehreetee
I don't know the Yugoslavian measures.	**Ja ne znam jugoslovenske mere.**	yah neh znahm yoogos**lo**vehnskeh **meh**reh

This is your size

Ladies

Dresses/suits						
American	10	12	14	16	18	20
British	32	34	36	38	40	42
Yugoslavian	38	40	42	44	46	48

Stockings							Shoes			
American } British	8	8½	9	9½	10	10½	6	7	8	9
Yugoslavian	0	1	2	3	4	5	36	38	38½	40

Gentlemen

Suits/overcoats							Shirts					
American } British	36	38	40	42	44	46	14	15	15½	16	16½	17
Yugoslavian	46	48	50	52	54	56	36	38	39	41	42	43

Shoes							
American } British	5	6	7	8	9	10	11
Yugoslavian	38	39	41	42	43	44	45

A good fit?

Can I try it on?	**Mogu li da probam?**	mogoo lee dah probahm
Where's the fitting room?	**Gde je soba za probavanje?**	gdeh yeh sobah zah probahvahneh
Is there a mirror?	**Imate li ogledalo?**	eemahteh lee oglehdahlo
Does it fit?	**Da li Vam odgovara?**	dah lee vahm odgovahrah

FOR NUMBERS, see page 175

It fits very well.	**Vrlo dobro mi odgovara.**	verlo dobro mee odgovahrah
It doesn't fit.	**Ne odgovara mi.**	neh odgovahrah mee
It's too...	**Suviše je...**	sooveesheh yeh
short/long	**kratko/dugačko**	krahtkoo/doogahchkoo
tight/loose	**tesno/široko**	tehsnoo/sheerokoo
How long will it take to alter?	**Koliko dugo treba da se to popravi?**	koleeko doogo trehbah dah seh to poprahvee

Shoes

I would like a pair of...	**Želeo bih par...**	zhehlebo beeh pahr
shoes	**cipela**	tseepehlah
sandals	**sandala**	sahndahlah
boots	**čizama**	cheezahmah
These are too...	**Ove su previše...**	oveh soo prehveesheh
narrow/wide	**uske/široke**	ooskeh/sheerokeh
large/small	**velike/male**	vehleekeh/mahlehneh
Do you have a larger size?	**Da li imate veći broj?**	dah lee eemahteh vehchee broy
I want a smaller size.	**Želeo bih manji broj.**	zhehleho beeh mahñee broy
Do you have the same in...?	**Da li imate iste u...?**	dah lee eemahteh eesteh oo
brown/beige	**braon/bež**	brahon/behzh
black/white	**crnom/belom**	tsernom/behlom

Shoes worn out? Here's the key to getting them fixed again:

Can you repair these shoes?	**Možete li popraviti ove cipele?**	mozhehteh lee poprahveetee oveh tseepehleh
Can you stitch this?	**Možete li ušiti ovo?**	mozhehteh lee oosheetee ovo
I want new soles and heels.	**Želeo bih nove djonove i pete.**	zhehleho beeh noveh jonoveh ee pehteh
When will they be ready?	**Kada će biti gotovo?**	kahdah cheh beetee gotovo

Clothes and accessories

I'd like a/an/some...	Želim...	zhehleem
anorak	vindjaknu	veendyahknoo
bathing cap	kapu za kupanje	kahpoo zah koopahñeh
bathrobe	bademantl	bahdehmahntl
bathing costume	kupaći kostim	koopahchee kosteem
bikini	bikini	beekeenee
blazer	bleizer	blehyzehr
blouse	bluzu	bloozoo
(rubber) boots	kaljače	kahlʸahcheh
bra	prslučić	persloocheech
braces (Br.)	tregere	trehgehreh
briefs	gaćice	gahcheetseh
cap	kapu	kahpoo
cape	kep	kehp
car coat	kaput za kola	kahpoot zah kolah
coat	kaput	kahpoot
dinner jacket	smoking	smokeeng
dress	haljinu	hahlʸeenoo
dressing gown	kućnu haljinu	koochnoo hahlʸeenoo
dungarees	radno odelo	rahdno odehlo
evening dress	večernju haljinu	vehchehrñoo hahlʸeenoo
frock	haljinu	hahlʸeenoo
fur coat	bundu	boondoo
garters	podvezice	podvehzeetseh
girdle	steznik	stehzneek
gloves	rukavice	rookahveetseh
handkerchief	maramicu	mahrahmeetsoo
hat	šešir	shehsheer
housecoat	kućni mantil	koochnee mahnteel
jacket	žaket	zhahkeht
jeans	farmerke	fahrmehrkeh
jersey	vunenu jaknu	voonehnoo yahknoo
jumper (Br.)	džemper	jehmpehr
knickers	pumperice	poompehreetseh
lingerie	ženski veš	zhehnskee vehsh
mackintosh	kišni kaput	keeshnee kahpoot
necktie	mašnu [kravatu]	mahshnoo [krahvahtoo]
nightdress	spavaćicu	spahvahcheetsoo
overalls	radni kombinezon	rahdnee kombeenehzon
panties	gaćice	gahcheetseh
pants (Am.)	pantalone	pahntahloneh
pants (Br.)	gaće	gahcheh
panty-girdle	mider gaćice	meedehr gahcheetseh
parka	vindjaknu	veendyahknoo

SHOPPING GUIDE

pullover	**pulover**	poolovehr
pyjamas	**pidžamu**	peejahmoo
raincoat	**kišni kaput**	keeshnee kahpoot
pair of sandals	**par sandala**	pahr sahndahlah
scarf	**šal**	shahl
shirt	**košulju**	koshoolʸoo
shoes	**cipele**	tseepehleh
shorts (Br.)	**šorc**	shorts
skirt	**suknju**	sookñoo
slacks	**pantalone [hlače]**	pahntahloneh [hlahcheh]
slip	**kombinezon**	kombeenehzon
slippers	**papuče**	pahpoocheh
sneakers	**patike**	pahteekeh
socks	**sokne**	sokneh
sports jacket	**sportski žaket**	sportskee zhahkeht
stockings	**ženske čarape**	zhehnskeh chahrahpeh
suit (men's)	**odelo**	odehlo
suit (women's)	**kostim**	kosteem
suspender belt	**kajiš**	kahyeesh
suspenders (Am.)	**tregere**	trehgehreh
tennis shoes	**patike za tenis**	pahteekeh zah tehnees
tights	**gimnastički kostim**	geemnahsteechkee kosteem
top coat	**kaput**	kahpoot
tracksuit	**trenerku**	trehnehrkoo
trousers	**pantalone [hlače]**	pahntahloneh [hlahsheh]
twin set	**set**	seht
underpants (men)	**muške gaće**	mooshkeh gahcheh
vest (Am.)	**prsluk**	perslook
vest (Br.)	**podkošulju**	podkoshoolʸoo
waistcoat	**prsluk**	perslook

belt	**kaiš**	kaheesh
button	**dugme**	doogmeh
collar	**kragna**	krahgnah
heel	**peta**	pehtah
lining	**postava**	postahvah
pocket	**džep**	jehp
shoe lace	**pertla**	pehrtlah
sole	**djon**	jon
zipper	**rajsferšlus**	rahysfehrshloos

Electrical appliances and accessories – Records

The voltage in Yugoslavia is 220 volts, 50 cycles A.C. Plugs are the common European type. An adaptor may prove useful.

What's the voltage?	**Kakav je napon ovde?**	kahkahv yeh nahpon ovdeh
I want a plug for this.	**Želim utikač za ovo.**	zhehleem ooteekahch zah ovo
Have you a battery for this?	**Imate li bateriju za ovo?**	eemahteh lee bahtehreeyoo zah ovo
This is broken. Can you repair it?	**Ovo se polomilo. Možete li popraviti?**	ovo seh polomeelo. mozhehteh lee poprahveetee
When will it be ready?	**Kad će biti gotovo?**	kahd cheh beetee gotovo
I'd like a/an/some...	**Želim...**	zhehleem
adaptor (for plug)	**adaptor**	ahdahptor
amplifier	**pojačivač**	poyahcheevahch
battery	**bateriju**	bahtehreeyoo
blender	**mikser**	meeksehr
clock	**sat**	saht
wall clock	**zidni sat**	zeednee saht
electric clock	**električni sat**	ehlehktreechnee saht
food mixer	**mikser**	meeksehr
hair drier	**fen za kosu**	fehn zah kosoo
iron	**peglu**	pehgloo
travelling iron	**putnu peglu**	pootnoo pehgloo
(electric) kettle	**(električni) lonac**	(ehlehktreechnee) lonahts
radio	**radio**	rahdeeo
car radio	**radio za kola**	rahdeeo zah kolah
portable radio	**portabl radio**	portahbl rahdeeo
record player	**gramofon**	grahmofon
portable	**portabl**	portahbl
shaver	**aparat za brijanje**	ahpahraht zah breeyahneh
speakers	**zvučnike**	zvoochneekeh
tape recorder	**magnetofon**	mahgnehtofon
for cassettes/ portable	**za kasete/portabl**	zah kahsehteh/portahbl
television	**televizijski aparat**	tehlehveezeeyskee ahpahraht
colour/portable	**u boji/portabl**	oo boyee/portahbl
toaster	**toster**	tostehr
transformer	**transformator**	trahnsformahtor

Records

Have you any records by...?	**Imate li ploče...?**	eemahteh lee plocheh
Can I listen to this record?	**Mogu li da čujem ovu ploču?**	mogoo lee dah chooyehm ovoo plochoo
I'd like a cassette.	**Želeo bih kasetu.**	zhehleho beeh kahsehtoo
I want a new needle.	**Želim novu iglu.**	zhehleem novoo eegloo

L.P.	**velika ploča**	vehleekah plochah
45 rpm	**45 okretaja**	chehterdehseht peht okrehtahyah
mono/stereo	**mono/stereo**	mono/stehreho

classical music	**klasična muzika**	klahseechnah moozeekah
folk music	**narodna muzika**	nahrodnah moozeekah
instrumental music	**instrumentalna muzika**	eenstroomehntahlnah moozeekah
jazz	**džez**	jehz
light music	**laka muzika**	lahkah moozeekah
orchestral music	**orkestarska muzika**	orkehstahrskah moozeekah
pop music	**pop muzika**	pop moozeekah

Men's hairdressing (barber)

I don't speak much Serbo-Croatian.	**Ne govorim dobro srpskohrvatski.**	neh govoreem dobro serpskohervahtskee
I'm in a terrible hurry.	**Strašno se žurim.**	strahshno seh zhooreem
I want a haircut, please.	**Hteo bih da se podšišam, molim Vas.**	hteho beeh dah seh podsheeshahm moleem vahs
I'd like a shave.	**Želeo bih da me obrijete.**	zhehleho beeh dah meh obreeyehteh
Don't cut it too short.	**Nemojte suviše visoko.**	nehmoyteh sooveesheh veesoko
Scissors only, please.	**Samo makazama, molim.**	sahmo mahkahzahmah moleem
A razor-cut, please.	**Britvom, molim.**	breetvom moleem
Don't use the clippers.	**Nemojte mašinom, molim Vas.**	nehmoyteh mahsheenom moleem vahs
Just a trim, please.	**Samo podšišajte, molim Vas.**	sahmo podsheeshahyteh moleem vahs
That's enough off.	**Dosta ste skinuli.**	dostah steh skeenoolee
A little more off the...	**Skinite još...**	skeeneeteh yosh
back	**pozadi**	pozahdee
neck	**na vratu**	nah vrahtoo
sides	**sa strane**	sah strahneh
top	**gore**	goreh
I don't want any cream.	**Ne želim nikakvu kremu.**	neh zhehleem neekahkvoo krehmoo
Don't use any oil, please.	**Ne želim ulje.**	neh zhehleem oolʸeh
Would you please trim my...?	**Podrežite, molim Vas...**	podrehzheeteh moleem vahs
beard	**bradu**	brahdoo
moustache	**brkove**	berkoveh
sideboards (sideburns)	**zulufi**	zooloofee
Thank you. That's fine.	**Hvala. Dobro je.**	hvahlah. dobro yeh
How much do I owe you?	**Koliko sam dužan?**	koleeko sahm doozhahn

SHOPPING GUIDE

FOR TIPPING, see page 1

Ladies' hairdressing

Can I make an appointment for some time on Thursday?	Da li mogu da zakažem za četvrtak?	dah lee mogoo dah zahkahzhehm zah chehtvertahk
I'd like it cut and shaped.	Želela bih da me ošišate i počešljate.	zhehlehlah beeh dah meh osheeshahteh ee pochehshlʸahteh
in a bun	pundja	poonjah
frizz style	kovrdže	koverjeh
fringe	šiške	sheeshkeh
page-boy style	rolna	rolnah
a razor cut	šišanje brijačem	sheeshahneh breeyahchehm
a restyle	novu frizuru	novoo freezooroo
with ringlets	šestice	shehsteetseh
with waves	talasi	tahlahsee
I want a...	Želim...	zhehleem
bleach	blajhanje	blahyhahñeh
colour rinse	preliv	prehleev
dye	farbanje	fahrbahñeh
permanent	trajnu ondulaciju	trahynoo ondoolahtseeyoo
tint	refleks	rehflehks
touch-up	popravak	poprahvahk
Do you have a colour chart?	Imate li pregled boja?	eemahteh lee prehglehd boyah
I want...	Želim...	zhehleem
the same colour	istu boju	eestoo boyoo
a darker colour	tamniju boju	tahmneeyoo boyoo
a lighter colour	svetliju boju	svehtleeyoo boyoo
auburn/blond/ brunette	kestenjasto/plavo/ brinet	kehstehñahsto/plahvo/ breeneht
Would you put this hair piece on for me?	Stavite mi molim Vas ovaj umetak od kose	stahveeteh mee moleem vahs ovahy oomehtahk od koseh
I don't want any hairspray.	Ne želim lak za kosu.	neh zhehleem lahk zah kosoo
I want a...	Želim...	zhehleem
manicure/pedicure/ face-pack	manikiranje/pedi-kiranje/masku	mahneekeerahñeh/ pehdeekeerahñeh/ mahskoo

FOR TIPPING, see page 1

SHOPPING GUIDE

Jeweller's – Watchmaker's

Can you repair this watch?	**Možete li popraviti ovaj sat?**	mozhehteh lee mee poprahveetee ovahy saht
The...is broken.	**...je polomljen.**	...yeh poloml'ehn
glass	**staklo**	stahklo
spring	**feder**	fehdehr
strap	**kaiš**	kaheesh
I want this watch cleaned.	**Možete li očistiti ovaj sat?**	mozhehteh lee ocheesteetee ovahy saht
When will it be ready?	**Kad će biti gotovo?**	kahd cheh beetee gotovo
Could I see that, please?	**Mogu li da vidim to, molim Vas?**	mogoo lee dah veedeem to moleem vahs
I'm just looking around.	**Samo bih malo razgledao.**	sahmo beeh mahlo rahzglehdaho
I want a small present for...	**Želim jedan mali poklon za...**	zhehleem yehdahn mahlee poklon zah
I don't want anything too expensive.	**Ne želim ništa suviše skupo.**	neh zhehleem neeshtah sooveesheh skoopo
I want something...	**Ja želim nešto...**	yah zhehleem nehshto
better	**bolje**	bol'eh
cheaper	**jeftinije**	yehfteeneeyeh
simpler	**jednostavnije**	yehdnostahvneeyeh
Is it real or imitation?	**Da li je pravo ili imitacija?**	dah lee yeh prahvo eelee eemeetahtseeyah
What is that stone?	**Kakav je to kamen?**	kahkahv yeh to kahmehn
Have you anything in gold?	**Imate li nešto od zlata?**	eemahteh lee nehshto od zlahtah
Is this real silver?	**Da li je ovo pravo srebro?**	dah lee yeh ovo prahvo srehbro

If it's made of gold, ask:

How many carats is this?	**Koliko ima karata?**	koleeko eemah kahrahtah

When you go to a jeweller's, you've probably got some idea of what you want beforehand. Find out what the article is made of and then look up its name in Serbo-Croatian in the following lists.

What's it made of?

amber	ćilibar	cheeleebahr
amethyst	ametist	ahmehteest
chromium	hrom	hrom
copper	bakar	bahkahr
coral	koral	korahl
cut glass	brušeno staklo	brooshehno stahklo
diamond	dijamant	deeyahmahnt
emerald	smaragd	smahrahgd
glass	staklo	stahklo
gold	zlato	zlahto
gold leaf	pozlaćen list	pozlahchehn leest
jade	žad	zhahd
onyx	aniks	ahneeks
pearl	biser	beesehr
pewter	kalaj [kositar]	kahlahy [koseetahr]
platinum	platina	plahteenah
ruby	rubin	roobeen
sapphire	safir	sahfeer
silver	srebro	srehbro
silver-plate	posrebren	posrehbrehn
stainless steel	nerdjajući čelik	neherjahyoochee chehleek
topaz	topaz	topahz
turquoise	tirkiz	teerkeez

What is it?

I'd like a/an/some…	Želim…	zhehleem
bangle	grivnu	greevnoo
beads	perle	pehrleh
bracelet	brezletnu	brehzlehtnoo
brooch	broš	brosh
chain	lanac	lahnahts
charm	mali ukras	mahlee ookrahs
cigarette case	kutiju za cigarete	kooteeyoo zah tseegahrehteh
cigarette lighter	upaljač	oopahlʸvahch
clip	broš	brosh

clock	sat	saht
alarm clock	budilnik	boodeelneek
travel alarm	sat za put	saht zah poot
collar stud	dugme za kragnu	doogmeh zah krahgnoo
cufflinks	dugmad za košulju	doogmahd zah koshool'oo
cutlery	pribor za jelo	preebor zah yehlo
earrings	mindjuše	meenjoosheh
jewel box	kutiju za nakit	kooteeyoo zah nahkeet
manicure set	manikir pribor	mahneekeer preebor
necklace	ogrlicu	ogerleetsoo
pendant	privesak	preevehsahk
pin	iglu	eegloo
powder compact	pudrijeru	poodreeyehroo
propelling pencil	višebojnu olovku	veeshehboynoo olovkoo
ring .	prsten	perstehn
engagement ring	veridbeni prsten	vehreedbehnee perstehn
signet ring	prsten sa pečatom	perstehn sah pehchahtom
wedding ring	venčani prsten [burma]	vehnchahnee perstehn [boormah]
rosary	brojanice	broyahneetseh
silverware	srebreno posudje	srehbrehno posoojeh
snuff box	burmuticu	boormooteetsoo
tie-clip	držač za kravatu	derzhach zah krahvahtoo
tie-pin	iglu za kravatu	eegloo zah krahvahtoo
vanity case	kutiju za kozmetiku	kooteeyoo zah kozmehteekoo
watch	sat	saht
pocket watch	džepni sat	jehpnee saht
with a second-hand	sa kazaljkom za sekunde	sah kahzahl'ekom zah sehkoondeh
wrist watch	ručni sat	roochnee saht
watch strap	kaiš za sat	kaheesh zah saht
chain strap	lanac za sat	lahnahts zah saht
leather strap	kožni kajiš	kozhnee kaheesh

Laundry – Dry cleaning

If your hotel doesn't have its own laundry/dry cleaning service, ask the porter:

SHOPPING GUIDE

Can you recommend a good dry cleaner?	**Možete li mi preporučiti dobru hemijsku čistionu?**	mozhehteh lee mee prehporoocheetee dobroo hehmeeyskoo cheesteeonoo
Where's the nearest laundry?	**Gde je najbliža radnja za pranje rublja?**	gdeh yeh nahybleezhah rahdnah zah prahñeh rooblʸah
I want these clothes...	**Želim ove stvari da se...**	zhehleem oveh stvahree dah seh
cleaned	**očiste**	ocheesteh
ironed	**ispeglaju**	eespehglahyoo
pressed	**ispeglaju**	eespehglahyoo
washed	**operu**	opehroo
When will it be ready?	**Kada će biti gotovo?**	kahdah cheh beetee gotovo
I need it...	**To mi treba...**	to mee trehbah
today	**danas**	dahnahs
tonight	**večeras**	vehchehrahs
tomorrow	**sutra**	sootrah
before Friday	**pre petka**	preh pehtkah
I want it as soon as possible.	**To mi treba što pre.**	to mee trehbah shto preh
Can you...this?	**Možete li mi ovo...?**	mozhehteh lee mee ovo
mend	**popraviti**	poprahveetee
patch	**zakrpiti**	zahkerpeetee
stitch	**zašiti**	zahsheetee
Can you sew on this button?	**Možete li mi zašiti ovo dugme?**	mozhehteh lee mee zahsheetee ovo doogmeh
Can you get this stain out?	**Možete li očistiti ovu fleku?**	mozhehteh lee mee ocheesteetee ovoo flehkoo
Can this be invisibly mended?	**Može li se ovo umetnički uštopati?**	mozheh lee seh ovo oomehtneechkee ooshtopahtee
This isn't mine.	**Ovo nije moje.**	ovo neeyeh moyeh
Where's my laundry? You promised it for today.	**Gde je moje rublje? Obećali ste za danas.**	gdeh yeh moyeh rooblʸeh? obehchahlee steh zah dahnahs

Photography

You can buy film everywhere in Yugoslavia but to be sure of having your favourite brand, and to save on cost, bring your own supply from home.

I want an inexpensive camera.	**Želim jednu ne previše skupu foto kameru.**	zhehleem yehdnoo neh prehveesheh skoopoo foto kahmehroo
Show me that one in the window.	**Pokažite mi onu u izlogu.**	pokahzheeteh mee onoo oo eezlogoo

Film

I'd like a film for this camera.	**Želim film za ovu kameru.**	zhehleem feelm zah ovoo kahmehroo
120 (6×6)	**stodvadeset**	stodvahdehseht
127 (4×4)	**stodvadeset sedam**	stodvahdehseht sehdahm
135 (24×36)	**stotrideset i pet**	stotreedehsehteepeht
8 mm	**od osam milimetera**	od osahm meeleemehtahrah
super 8	**super osam**	soopehr osahm
35 mm	**od trideset pet milimetera**	od treedehseht peht meeleemehtahrah
620 (6×6) roll film	**šest stotina dvadeset rol film**	shehst stoteenah dvahdehseht rol feelm
20/36 exposures	**dvadeset/trideset šest snimaka**	dvahdehseht/treedehsehteeshehst sneemahkah
this size	**ovu dimenziju**	ovoo deemehnzeeyoo
this ASA/DIN number	**ovaj ASA/DIN broj**	ovahy ahsah/deen broy
black and white	**crno/beli**	tserno/behlee
colour	**u boji [kolor]**	oo boyee [kolor]
colour negative	**kolor negativ**	kolor nehgahteev
colour reversal	**kolor umker**	kolor oomkehr
colour slide (transparency)	**kolor dijapozitiv**	kolor deeyahpozeeteev
artificial light type (indoor)	**za veštačko svetlo**	zah vehshtahchko svehtlo
daylight type (outdoor)	**za dnevno svetlo**	zah dnehvno svehtlo
fast	**brzi**	berzee
fine-grain	**fino-zrnasti**	feeno zernahstee
Does the price include processing?	**Da li je u cenu uračunato razvijanje?**	dah lee yeh oo tsehnoo oorahchoonahto rahzveeyahneh

FOR NUMBERS, see page 175

Processing

How much do you charge for developing?	**Koliko naplaćujete za razvijanje?**	koleeko nah**plah**chooyehteh zah rahzvee**ya**hneh
I want... prints of each negative.	**Želim po...slika od svakog negativa.**	zhehleem po...**slee**kah od svahkog **neh**gahteevah
Will you enlarge this, please?	**Možete li mi ovo povećati, molim Vas?**	**mozh**ehteh lee mee **ovo** povehchahtee **mo**leem vahs

Accessories

I want a/an/some...	**Želim...**	zhehleem
cable release	**žičani okidač**	zheechahnee o**kee**dach
exposure meter	**svetlomer**	**sveh**tlomehr
flash bulbs	**sijalice za fleš**	seeyahleetseh zah flehsh
flash cubes	**fleš kockice**	flehsh **kots**keetseh
for black and white	**za crno/beli**	zah **tser**no/**beh**lee
for colour	**za kolor**	zah kolor
filter	**filter**	**feel**tehr
red/yellow	**crveni/žuti**	tser**veh**nee/**zhoo**tee
ultra violet	**ultra violet**	**ool**trahveeoleht
lens	**sočivo**	**so**cheevo
lens cap	**poklopac za sočivo**	poklopahts zah socheevoo
lens cleaners	**sredstvo za čišćenje sočiva**	**srehd**stvo zah **cheesh**chehñeh **so**cheevah
tripod	**nogare [stativ]**	**no**gahreh [**staht**eev]

This camera doesn't work. Can you repair it?	**Ova kamera je pokvarena. Možete li je popraviti?**	ovah **kah**mehrah yeh pokvahrehnah. **mozh**ehteh lee yeh poprahveetee
The film is jammed.	**Film se zaglavio.**	feelm seh zah**glah**veeo
There's something wrong with the...	**Nešto nije u redu sa...**	**nehsh**to **nee**yeh oo **reh**doo sah
exposure counter	**brojačem snimaka**	broyah**chehm snee**mahkah
film winder	**navijačem filma**	nahveeyah**chehm** feelmah
light meter	**svetlomerom**	**sveh**tlomehrom
rangefinder	**daljinomerom**	**dah**l'eenomehrom

Provisions

Here's a basic list of food and drink that you might want on a picnic or for the occasional meal at home.

I'd like a/an/some...	Želim...	zhehleem
apples	jabuke	yahbookeh
bananas	banane	bahnahneh
biscuits	keks	kehks
bread	hleb [kruh]	hlehb [krooh]
butter	puter	pootehr
cake	kolače	kolahcheh
cheese	sir	seer
chocolate	čokoladu	chokolahdoo
coffee	kafu	kahfoo
cold meat	hladno meso [narezak]	hlahdno mehso [nahrehzahk]
cookies	keks	kehks
crackers	slani keks	slahnee kehks
cucumber	krastavce	krahstahvtseh
frankfurters	kobasice	kobahseetseh
french fries	pomfrit	pomfreet
ham	šunku	shoonkoo
hamburgers	faširane šnicle	fahsheerahneh shneetsleh
ice-cream	sladoled	slahdolehd
lemonade	limunadu	leemonahdoo
lemons	limunove	leemoonoveh
lettuce	zelenu salatu	zehlehnoo sahlahtoo
liver sausage	jetrene kobasice	yehtrehneh kobahseetseh
luncheon meat	mesni doručak	mehsnee doroochahk
milk	mleko	mlehko
mustard	senf	sehnf
oranges	pomorandže	pomorahnjeh
orange squash (drink)	sok od pomorandže	sok od pomorahnjeh
pâté	paštetu od džigerice	pahshtehtoo od jeegehreetseh
pepper	biber [papar]	beebehr [pahpahr]
pickles	turšiju [kiselu salatu]	toorsheeyoo [keesehloo sahlahtoo]
pork	svinjetinu	sveeñehteenoo
potato chips	pomfrit	pomfreet
potatoes	krompir	krompeer
rolls	kifle	keefleh
salad	salatu	sahlahtoo
salami	salamu	sahlahmoo
sandwiches	sendviče	sehndveecheh
sausages	kobasice	kobahseetseh

sugar	šećer	shehchehr
sweets	slatkiše	slahtkeesheh
tea	čaj	chahy
tomatoes	paradajz	pahrahdahyz
tongue	jezik	yehzeek
veal	teletinu	tehlehteenoo

And don't forget...

a bottle opener	otvarač za flaše	otvahrahch zah flahsheh
a corkscrew	vadičep	vahdeechehp
matches	šibice	sheebeetseh
(paper) napkins	(papirnate) salvete	(pahpeernahteh) sahlvehteh
a can opener	otvarač za konzerve	otvahrahch zah konzehrveh

Weights and measures

1 kilogram or kilo (kg) = 1000 grams (g)

| 100 g = 3.5 oz. | ½ kg = 1.1 lb. |
| 200 g = 7.0 oz. | 1 kg = 2.2 lb. |

1 oz. = 28.35 g
1 lb. = 453.60 g

---

1 liter (l) = 0.88 imp. quarts = 1.06 U.S. quarts

| 1 imp. quart = 1.14 l | 1 U.S. quart = 0.95 l |
| 1 imp. gallon = 4.55 l | 1 U.S. gallon = 3.8 l |

---

barrel	bure	booreh
box	kutija	kooteeyah
can	konzerva	konzehrvah
carton	pakovanje	pahkovahñeh
crate	sanduk	sahndook
jar	tegla	tehglah
pack(et)	paket	pahkeht
tin	konzerva	konzehrvah
tube	tuba	toobah

Souvenirs

Any hand-made object, generally speaking, can be of interest
to a souvenir or antique hunter. There's still a lot of local handi-
craft in Yugoslavia, and you'll discover many nicely decorated
objects destined for daily use, which you may wish to buy as a
souvenir or a gift. Hand-carved brass dishes and cups, painted
shawls and other tissues, and wood-carvings in particular are
available everywhere and are excellent value for the money
spent. Given below is a list of articles with their names in
Serbo-Croatian.

Do you have…?	Imate li…?	eemahteh lee
baskets	košare	koshahreh
copperwork	izradjene predmete od bakra	eezrahjehneh **prehd**mehteh od **bah**krah
dolls in national costume	lutke u narodnim nošnjama	lootkeh oo **nah**rodneem noshñahmah
earthenware	lončarske predmete	lonchahrskeh **prehd**mehteh
embroidery	vezovi	vehzovee
hand-made carpets	ćilime pravljene rukom	cheeleemeh prahvlˑvehneh rookom
hand-made national costumes	narodne nošnje	nahrodneh noshñeh
hand-made wooden plates	izradjene drvene tanjire	eezrahjehneh **der**vehneh tahñeereh
hand-made woodwork	izradjene drvene predmete	eezrahjehneh **der**vehneh **prehd**mehteh
leather drinking flasks	flaše presvučene kožom	flahsheh prehsvoochehneh kozhom
Macedonian caps	fesove	fehsoveh
musical instruments	narodne muzičke instrumente	nahrodneh **mooz**eechkeh eenstroo**meh**nteh
sea coral	koralje	korahlˑveh
seashells	školjke	shkolˑvkeh
Serbian moccassins	opanke	opahnkeh
silverwork	ručne radove od srebra	roochneh **rah**doveh od **sreh**brah
shepherd's bags	seljačke torbe	sehlˑvahchkeh torbeh
Turkish coffee pots	turske džezve	toorskeh jehzveh
Turkish coffee sets	turske servise za kafu	toorskeh seh**rvee**seh zah kahfoo
wooden pipes	drvene lule	**der**vehneh looleh

Tobacconist's

Yugoslavian cigarettes come in a strong, black Turkish variety
as well as in mild blends similar to western European cigarettes. In addition to many local makes, certain American
brands are manufactured in Yugoslavia under licence.

Give me a/an/some... please.	Dajte mi molim...	dahyteh mee moleem
box of...	kutiju...	kooteeyoo
cigars	cigara	tseegahrah
cigarette case	tabakeru	tahbahkehroo
cigarette holder	cigaršpic	tseegahrshpeets
cigarette lighter	upaljač	oopahlʸahch
flints	kremenove	krehmehnoveh
lighter	upaljač	oopahlʸahch
lighter fluid/gas	benzin/plin za upaljač	behnzeen/pleen zah oopahlʸahch
refill for a lighter	punjenje za upaljač	pooñehñeh zah oopahlʸahch
matches	šibice	sheebeetseh
packet of cigarettes	kutiju cigareta	kooteeyoo tseegahrehtah
packet of Drina	kutiju Drine	kooteeyoo dreeneh
pipe	lulu	looloo
pipe tobacco	duvana za lulu	doovahnah zah looloo
pipe cleaners	čistač za lulu	cheestahch zah looloo
tobacco pouch	kesu za duvan	kehsoo zah doovahn
wick	fitilj	feeteelʸ
Have you any...?	Imate li...?	eemahteh lee
American cigarettes	američke cigarete	ahmehreechkee tseegahrehteh
English cigarettes	engleske cigarete	ehnglehskeh tseegahrehteh
menthol cigarettes	mentol cigarete	mehntol tseegahrehteh
I'll take two packets.	Uzeću dve kutije.	oozehchoo dveh kooteeyeh
I'd like a carton.	Želim pakovanje od deset kutija.	zhehleem pahkovahñeh od dehseht kooteeyah

filter-tipped	sa filterom	sah feeltehrom
without filter	bez filtera	behz feeltehrah

And while we're on the subject of cigarettes, suppose you want to offer somebody one?

Would you like a cigarette?	**Izvolite cigaretu.**	eezvoleeteh tseegahrehtoo
Have one of mine.	**Izvolite jednu od mene.**	eezvoleeteh **yeh**dnoo od **meh**neh
Try one of these. They're very mild.	**Probajte jednu od ovih. Vrlo su blage.**	probahyteh **yeh**dnoo od oveeh. **ver**lo soo **blah**geh
They're a bit strong.	**Previše su jake.**	prehvee**sheh** soo **yah**keh

And if somebody offers you one?

Thank you.	**Hvala.**	**hvah**lah
No, thanks.	**Ne, hvala.**	neh **hvah**lah
I don't smoke.	**Ne pušim.**	neh **poo**sheem
I've given it up.	**Prestao sam da pušim.**	preh**stah**o sahm dah **poo**sheem

TOBACCONIST'S

Your money: banks — currency

In banks in the larger towns, there's sure to be someone who speaks English. In most tourist centres, you'll find small currency-exchange offices (*Menjačnice*–**meh**ñahchneetseh) with notices and signs in English.

Try to assess how much dinar cash you will need, because excess cash cannot be reconverted.

Banking hours

In the larger centres banks are generally open from 8 a.m. to noon and from 1 to 7 p.m., Monday to Friday, and from 8 a.m. to noon on Saturdays. When banks are closed or too far away, you can change money at identical rates in authorized currency-exchange offices including travel agencies and hotels.

Monetary unit

The monetary unit of Yugoslavia is the *dinar* (abbreviated *din.*). Sometimes the dinar is referred to as *novi dinar* (new dinar). In conversation, Yugoslavs may refer to *stari dinar* (old dinar), 100 of which make a new dinar.

Coins: 1, 2, 5, 10, 50, 100 dinars.
Banknotes: 10, 20, 50, 100, 500, 1,000, 5,000, 20,000 dinars.

Credit cards and traveller's cheques

Although many hotels, restaurants and tourist-oriented enterprises accept credit cards, they're by no means known everywhere, particularly in the villages.

Traveller's cheques may be changed at banks, hotels and travel agencies and are accepted in many shops and restaurants.

Before going

Where's the nearest bank/currency-exchange office?	Gde je najbliža banka/menjačnica?	gdeh yeh **nahy**bleezhah **bahn**kah/**meh**ñahchneetsah
Where can I cash a traveller's cheque (check)?	Gde mogu da promenim putni ček?	gdeh **mo**goo dah pro**mehn**eem **poot**nee chehk
Where's the American Express?	Gde je Ameriken expres?	gdeh yeh ah**meh**reekehn ehk**sprehs**

Inside

I want to change some dollars.	Želim da promenim dolare.	**zheh**leem dah pro**mehn**eem **do**lahreh
I'd like to change some pounds.	Želim da promenim funte.	**zheh**leem dah pro**mehn**eem **foon**teh
Here's my passport	Izvolite moj pasoš.	eez**vo**leeteh moy **pah**sosh
What's the exchange rate?	Kakav je kurs?	**kah**kahv yeh koors
What rate of commission do you charge?	Kolika je vaša provizija?	ko**lee**kah yeh **vah**shah pro**vee**zeeyah
Can you cash a personal cheque?	Možete li promeniti jedan ček?	**mozh**ehteh lee pro**mehn**eetee **yeh**dahn chehk
How long will it take to clear?	Koliko će trajati dok se proveri?	ko**lee**ko cheh **trah**yahtee dok seh pro**veh**ree
Can you cable my bank?	Možete li da telegrafišete mojoj banci?	**mozh**ehteh lee dah tehleh**grah**feeshehteh **mo**yoy **bahn**tsee
I have...	Ja imam...	yah **ee**mahm
a letter of credit	kreditno pismo	**kreh**deetno **pee**smo
an introduction from...	preporuku od...	preh**po**rookoo od
a credit card	kreditnu kartu	**kreh**deetnoo **kahr**too
I'm expecting some money from...Has it arrived yet?	Očekujem novac iz...Da li je već stigao?	o**chehk**ooyehm **no**vahts eez... dah lee yeh vehch **stee**gaho
Give me...100-dinar notes (bills) and some small change, please.	Dajte mi, molim Vas,...novčanice od 100 dinara i nešto sitnine.	**dahy**teh mee **mo**leem vahs... **nov**chahneetseh od 100 **dee**nahrah ee **nehsh**to **seet**neeneh

FOR NUMBERS, see page 175

BANKS

| Give me...large notes and the rest in small notes. | **Dajte mi...krupnih novčanica a ostalo u malim novčanicama.** | dahyteh mee...**kroopneeh** novchahneetsah ah ostahlo oo mahleem **novchahnee**-tsahmah |
| Could you check that again, please? | **Možete li to da proverite još jednom, molim Vas?** | mozhehteh lee to dah provehreeteh yosh **yeh**dnom moleem vahs |

BANKS

Currency converter

In a world of fluctuating currencies, we can offer you no more than this do-it-yourself chart. You can get a card showing current exchange rates from banks, travel agents, tourist offices, etc. But why not fill in this chart, too, for handy reference?

Dinars	£	$
1		
2		
5		
10		
20		
50		
75		
100		
500		
1,000		

At the post office

The business hours of post offices in Yugoslavia vary, depending on the size of the town and the counter you want. Normally, it's from 8 a.m. through to 8 p.m. In major cities, there's always at least one post office where you can send cables, etc., until midnight. Stamps are also sold at tobacconist's shops.

Mail boxes in Yugoslavia are painted yellow. They are affixed on house walls, usually at street corners.

Where's the nearest post office?	**Gde je najbliža pošta?**	gdeh yeh **nahy**bleezhah poshtah
Can you tell me how I get to the post office?	**Možete li mi reći kako ću doći do pošte?**	**mo**zhehteh lee mee **re**chee **kah**ko choo **do**chee do poshteh
What time does the post office open/close?	**Kad se pošta otvara/zatvara?**	kahd seh poshtah **ot**vahrah/**zaht**vahrah
Which window do I go to for stamps?	**Na kome šalteru se prodaju marke?**	nah **ko**meh **shahl**tehroo seh **pro**dahyoo **mahr**keh
At which counter can I cash an international money order?	**Na kome šalteru mogu unovčiti internacionalnu novčanu uputnicu?**	nah **ko**meh **shahl**tehroo **mo**goo oonov**chee**tee eentehrnahtseeonahlnoo **nov**chahnoo oopootneetsoo
I want some stamps, please.	**Želeo bih nešto poštanskih maraka, molim Vas.**	**zhehl**eho beeh **neh**shto poshtahnskeeh **mahr**ahkah moleem vahs
I want...10-dinar stamps and...5-dinar stamps.	**Želim...maraka od 10 dinara i... marke od 5 dinara.**	**zhehl**eem...**mahr**ahkah od 10 **deen**ahrah ee... **mahr**keh od 5 **deen**ahrah
What's the postage for a letter to...?	**Kolika je poštarina za pismo za...?**	**koleekah** yeh posh**tah**reenah zah **pees**mo zah
What's the postage for a postcard to England?	**Kolika je poštarina za dopisnicu za Englesku?**	**koleekah** yeh posh**tah**reenah zah **ehn**glehskoo
When will this letter get there?	**Kad će ovo pismo stići tamo?**	kahd cheh ovo **pees**mo **stee**chee tahmo

FOR NUMBERS, see page 175

Do all letters go airmail?	Da li sva pisma idu avionom?	dah lee svah peesmah eedoo ahveeonom
I want to send this parcel.	Želim da pošaljem ovaj paket.	zhehleem dah poshahlʸehm ovahy pahkeht
Do I need to fill in a customs declaration?	Da li trebam da ispunim carinsku deklaraciju?	dah lee trehbahm dah eespooneem tsahreenskoo dehklahrahtseeyoo
I want to register this letter.	Želim da pošaljem ovo pismo preporučeno.	zhehleem dah poshahlʸehm ovo peesmo prehporoochehno
Where's the letter-box?	Gde je poštansko sanduče?	gdeh yeh poshtahnsko sahndoocheh
I want to send this by...	Ovo želim da pošaljem	ovo zhehleem dah poshahlʸehm
airmail	avionom	ahveeonom
express (special delivery)	ekspres	ehksprehs
recorded delivery	s povratnim recepisom	s povrahtneem rehtsehpeesom
registered mail	preporučeno	prehporoochehno
Where is the poste restante (general delivery)?	Gde je poste restant?	gdeh yeh posteh rehstahnt
Is there any mail for me? My name is...	Ima li pošte za mene? Ja se zovem...	eemah lee poshteh zah mehneh yah seh zovehm
Here's my passport.	Izvolite moj pasoš.	eezvoleeteh moy pahsosh

POŠTANSKE MARKE	STAMPS
PAKETI	PARCELS
NOVČANE POŠILJKE	MONEY ORDERS

Cables (telegrams)

| Where's the nearest cable office? | Gde je najbliža pošta za brzojave? | gdeh yeh nahybleezhah poshtah zah berzoyahveh |
| I want to send a cable (telegram). May I have a form, please? | Želim da pošaljem telegram. Molim Vas formular. | zhehleem dah poshahlʸehm tehlehgrahm. moleem vahs formoolahr |

How much is it per word?	**Koliko košta jedna reč?**	koleeko koshtah yehdnah rehch
How long will a cable to Boston take?	**Koliko treba da telegram stigne u Boston?**	koleeko trehbah dah tehlehgrahm steegneh oo boston
Send it collect.	**Pošaljite na njihov račun.**	poshahlʸeeteh nah ñeehov rahchoon

Telephoning

Most towns have telephones on the street from which you may dial local calls by depositing 2 dinars. For long-distance calls, the telephone office is located in the local post office. In most localities in Yugoslavia, you can dial direct to western Europe. Or, if you prefer, your hotel switchboard should be able to handle any calls, local or international.

Where's the telephone?	**Gde je telefon?**	gdeh yeh tehlehfon
Where's the nearest telephone booth?	**Gde je najbliža telefonska govornica?**	gdeh yeh nahybleezhah tehlehfonskah govorneetsah
May I use your phone?	**Mogu li se poslužiti Vašim telefonom?**	mogoo lee seh posloozheetee vahsheem tehlehfonom
Have you a telephone directory for...?	**Imate li telefonski imenik za...?**	eemahteh lee tehlehfonskee eemehneek zah
Can you help me get this number?	**Hoćete li mi nazvati ovaj broj?**	hochehteh lee mee nahzvahteh ovahy broy

Operator

Do you speak English?	**Govorite li engleski?**	govoreeteh lee ehnglehskee
Good morning. I want Belgrade 123-456.	**Dobro jutro. Trebam Beograd 123-456.**	dobro yootro. trehbahm behograhd 123-456.
Can I dial direct?	**Mogu li direktno nazvati?**	mogoo lee deerehktno nahzvahteh
I want to reverse the charges.	**Želim da govorim na račun druge strane.**	zhehleem dah govoreem nah rahchoon droogeh strahneh
Will you tell me the cost of the call afterwards?	**Kažite mi cenu razgovora posle.**	kahzheeteh mee tsehnoo rahzgovorah posleh

Speaking

I want to speak to...	Želim da govorim sa...	zhehleem dah govoreem sah
Would you put me through to...?	Hoćete li mi dati vezu sa...?	hochehteh lee mee dahtee vehzoo zah
I want extension...	Ja želim lokal...	yah zhehleem lokahl
Is that...?	Da li je to...?	dah lee yeh to
Hello. This is...	Halo, ovde...	hahlo ovdeh

Bad luck

Would you try again later, please?	Molim Vas, hoćete li pokušati kasnije ponovno?	moleem vahs hochehteh lee pokooshahtee kahsneeyeh ponovno
Operator, you gave me the wrong number.	Gospodjice, dali ste mi pogrešan broj.	gospojeetseh dahlee steh mee pogrehshahn broy

Telephone alphabet

A	Avala	ahvahlah	M	Mostar	mostahr
B	Beograd	behograhd	N	Niš	neesh
C	Cetinje	tsehteeñeh	Nj	Njegoš	nehgosh
Č	Čačak	chahchahk	O	Osijek	oseeyehk
Ć	Ćuprija	choopreeyah	P	Pirot	peerot
D	Dubrovnik	doobrovneek	R	Rijeka	reeyehkah
Dj	Djakovo	jahkovo	S	Skopje	skopyeh
Dž	Džamija	jahmeeyah	Š	Šibenik	sheebehneek
E	Evropa	ehvropah	T	Titograd	teetograhd
F	Foča	fochah	U	Uroševac	ooroshehvats
G	Gorica	goreetsah	V	Valjevo	vahlʸehvo
H	Hercegovina	hehrtsehgoveenah	Z	Zagreb	zahgrehb
I	Istra	eestrah	Ž	Žirovnica	zheerovneetsah
J	Jadran	yahdrahn	Q	Kvadrat	kvahdraht
K	Kosovo	kosovo	W	Duplo V	dooplo veh
L	Lika	leekah	Y	Ipsilon	eepseelon
Lj	Ljubljana	lʸooblʸahnah	X	Iks	eeks

Not there

When will he be back?	**Kad će se vratiti?**	kahd cheh seh **vrah**teetee
Will you tell him I called? My name's...	**Recite mu da sam ga tražio, molim Vas. Ja se zovem...**	**reht**seeteh moo dah sahm gah **trah**zheeo **mo**leem vahs. yah seh zo**vehm**
Would you ask him to call me?	**Zamolite ga da me nazove.**	zah**mo**leeteh gah dah meh nah**zo**veh
Would you take a message, please?	**Da li mogu da ostavim poruku, molim Vas?**	dah lee **mo**goo dah **o**stahveem po**roo**koo **mo**leem vahs

Charges

What's the cost of that call?	**Koliko košta taj razgovor?**	ko**lee**eko **ko**shtah tahy **rah**zgovor
I want to pay for the call.	**Želim da platim razgovor.**	**zheh**leem dah **plah**teem **rah**zgovor

Possible answers

Telefon za vas.	There's a telephone call for you.
Trebaju Vas na telefon.	You're wanted on the telephone.
Koji broj zovete?	What number are you calling?
Linija je zauzeta.	The line's engaged.
Nema odgovora.	There's no answer.
Nazvali ste pogrešan broj.	You've got the wrong number.
Telefon je pokvaren.	The phone is out of order.
Trenutno nije ovde.	He's out at the moment.

The car

We'll start this section by considering your possible needs at a filling station. Most filling stations don't handle major repairs; but apart from provisioning you with fuel, they may be helpful in solving all kinds of minor problems.

Where's the nearest filling station?	**Gde je najbliža benzinska stanica?**	gdeh yeh **nahy**bleezhah **behn**zeenskah **stahn**eetsah
I want… litres, please.	**Želim… litara, molim.**	**zheh**leem… **lee**tahrah moleem
ten/twenty/fifty	**deset/dvadeset/ pedeset**	**deh**seht/**dvah**dehseht/ pe**deh**seht
I want 15 litres of standard/premium.	**Želim 15 litara premiuma/ supera.**	**zheh**leem 15 **lee**tahrah prehmeeoomah/ soopehrah
Full tank, please.	**Napunite molim.**	nah**poo**neeteh moleem
Check the oil, please.	**Proverite ulje, molim Vas.**	pro**veh**reeteh ool^yeh moleem vahs
Check the water, please.	**Molim Vas proverite vodu.**	moleem vahs pro**veh**reeteh vodoo
Top up (fill up) the battery with distilled water.	**Napunite akumulator destilovanom vodom.**	nah**poo**neeteh ahkoomoolahtor **dehs**teelovahnom vodom
Put in some anti-freeze, please.	**Stavite antifriz, molim Vas.**	**stah**veeteh ahnteefreez moleem vahs
Check the brake fluid.	**Kontrolišite ulje za kočnice.**	kontro**lee**sheeteh ool^yeh zah **koch**neetseh

Fluid measures					
litres	imp. gal.	U.S. gal.	litres.	imp. gal.	U.S. gal.
5	1.1	1.3	30	6.6	7.8
10	2.2	2.6	35	7.7	9.1
15	3.3	3.9	40	8.8	10.4
20	4.4	5.2	45	9.9	11.7
25	5.5	6.5	50	11.0	13.0

FOR NUMBERS, see page 175

Tire pressure			
lb./sq. in.	kg/cm²	lb./sq. in.	kg/cm²
10	0.7	26	1.8
12	0.8	27	1.9
15	1.1	28	2.0
18	1.3	30	2.1
20	1.4	33	2.3
21	1.5	36	2.5
23	1.6	38	2.7
24	1.7	40	2.8

Would you check the tires?	**Proverite, molim Vas, gume.**	provehreeteh moleem vahs goomeh
The pressure should be one point six front, one point eight rear.	**Pritisak mora biti: jedan koma šest prednje, jedan koma osam zadnje gume.**	preeteesahk morah beetee: yehdahn komah shehst prehdñeh yehdahn komah osahm zahdñeh goomeh
Check the spare tire, too, please.	**Proverite rezervnu gumu takodje, molim Vas.**	provehreeteh rehzehrvnoo goomoo tahkojeh moleem vahs
Can you fix this flat (mend this puncture)?	**Možete li zakrpiti ovu gumu?**	mozhehteh lee mee zahkerpeetee ovoo goomoo
Will you change this tire, please?	**Hoćete li promeniti ovu gumu, molim Vas?**	hochehteh lee mee promehneetee ovoo goomoo
Would you clean the windshield (windscreen)?	**Molim Vas očistite šoferšajbnu.**	moleem vahs ocheesteeteh shofehrshahybnoo
Have you a road map of this district?	**Imate li autokartu [kartu autoputeva] ove oblasti?**	eemahteh lee ahootokahrtoo [kahrtoo pootehvah] oveh oblahstee
Where's the ladies'/men's toilet?	**Gde je toalet za žene/muškarce?**	gdeh yeh toahleht zah zhehneh/mooshkahrtseh

Asking the way – Street directions

Excuse me.	Izvinite.	eezveeneeteh
Can you tell me the way to...?	Možete li mi pokazati put za...?	mozhehteh lee mee pokahzahtee poot zah
How do I get to...?	Kako mogu da dodjem do...?	kahko mogoo dah dojehm do
Where does this road lead to?	Kuda vodi ovaj put?	koodah vodee ovahy poot
Can you show me on this map where I am?	Možete li mi pokazati na ovoj karti gde se nalazim?	mozhehteh lee mee pokahzahtee nah ovoy kahrtee gdeh seh nahlahzeem
How far is it to... from here?	Koliko je odavde do...?	koleeko yeh odahvdeh do

Miles into kilometres

1 mile=1.609 kilometres (km)

miles	10	20	30	40	50	60	70	80	90	100
km	16	32	48	64	80	97	113	129	145	161

Kilometres into miles

1 kilometre (km)=0.62 miles

km	10	20	30	40	50	60	70	80	90	100	110	120	130
miles	6	12	19	25	31	37	44	50	56	62	68	75	81

Possible answers

Vi ste na pogrešnom putu.	You're on the wrong road.
Idite pravo.	Go straight ahead.
To je tamo na levoj (desnoj) strani.	It's down there on the left (right).
Idite tim putem.	Go that way.
Idite do prve (druge) raskrsnice.	Go to the first (second) crossroads.
Skrenite levo (desno) kod semafora.	Turn left (right) at the traffic lights.

In the rest of this section we'll be more closely concerned with the car itself. We have divided it into two parts:

Part A contains general advice on motoring in Yugoslavia, hints and regulations. It's essentially for reference, and is therefore to be browsed over, preferable in advance.

Part B is concerned with the practical details of accidents, breakdown and emergency. It includes a list of car parts and a list of things that may go wrong with them. All you have to do is to show it to the garage mechanic and get him to point to the items required.

Part A

Customs-Documentation

You will require the following documents:

    passport
    international insurance certificate (green card)
    car registration certificate
    valid home driving licence

The nationality plate or sticker must be on the car.

In Yugoslavia, you can drive with a British or American driving licence. But if you plan to visit other countries, check whether an international permit is required.

Motorists are required to have in their vehicle a spare set of bulbs and a reflector warning triangle for use in case of breakdown. The use of seat belts is obligatory. Crash helmets are compulsory for both riders and passengers on motorcycles and scooters.

Here's my...	Izvolite moju...	eezvoleeteh moyoo
driving licence	vozačku dozvolu	vozahchkoo dozvoloo
green card	zelenu kartu	zehlehnoo kahrtoo
passport	pasoš	pahsosh
I haven't anything to declare.	Nemam ništa da prijavim za carinu.	nehmahm neeshtah dah preeyahveem zah tsahreenoo
I've...	Imam...	eemahm
a carton of cigarettes	deset kutija cigareta	dehseht kooteeyah tseegahrehtah
a bottle of whisky	flašu viskija	flahshoo veeskeeyah
a bottle of wine	flašu vina	flahshoo veenah
We're staying for...	Ostajemo...	ostahyehmo
a week	nedelju dana	nehdehlʸoo dahnah
two weeks	dve nedelje	dveh nehdehlʸeh
a month	mesec dana	mehsehts dahnah

Roads

The classification of roads in Yugoslavia is as follows:

Autoput
(ahootopoot)
motorway (expressway)

Glavni tranzitni put
(glahvnee trahnzeetnee poot)
main road (highway)

Sporedni put
(sporehdnee poot)
secondary road

Lokalni put
(lokahlnee poot)
local road

In some areas of the country the word *cesta* (**tseh**stah) is substituted for *put*.

Remember to drive on the right and overtake on the left. The casualty rate on the roads in Yugoslavia is high. Drivers should pay special attention and drive carefully.

Traffic offences

The police can fine you on the spot. A small fine must be paid immediately or mailed promptly. You can opt to go before a local traffic court; but this can be time-consuming.

In case of serious trouble, insist on an interpreter.

I'm sorry, officer. I didn't see the sign/light.	**Izvinite. Nisam video znak/svetlo.**	eezvee**nee**teh. **nee**sahm **vee**deho znahk/**sveh**tlo
I didn't realise my speed.	**Nisam primetio da tako brzo vozim.**	**nee**sahm pree**meh**teeo dah **tah**ko **ber**zo vo**zeem**
Here's my name and address.	**Izvolite moje ime i adresu.**	eezvo**lee**teh **moy**eh **ee**meh ee ah**dreh**soo

Parking

Use your common sense when parking. The police (*milicija*–**mee**leetseeyah) are normally reasonably lenient with tourists, but don't push your luck too far.

Park your car in the direction of moving traffic on the right-hand side of the road, not against the flow of traffic.

Obey the parking regulations, which will be indicated by signs or by lines painted on the sidewalks. In many cities in Yugoslavia, you may park your car on the sidewalk, even in the downtown area.

Excuse me. Can I park here?	**Izvinite. Mogu li da parkiram kola ovde?**	eezvee**nee**teh. **mo**goo lee dah pahr**kee**rahm kolah ovdeh
How long can I park here?	**Koliko dugo mogu da ostavim kola ovde?**	**ko**leeko **doo**go **mo**goo dah **os**tahveem kolah ovdeh
What's the charge for parking here?	**Koliko se ovde naplaćuje za parkiranje?**	**ko**leeko seh ovdeh nah**plah**chooyeh zah pahr**kee**rahñeh
Do I have to leave my lights on?	**Treba li da ostavim svetla upaljena?**	**treh**bah lee dah **os**tahveem **sveh**tlah oopahl'**eh**nnah

CAR – INFORMATION

Yugoslavian road signs

Here are some of the main signs and notices you're likely to
encounter when driving in Yugoslavia. Obviously, they should
be studied in advance. You can't drive and read at the same
time!

AERODROM	Airport
AUTOMEHANIČAR	Car mechanic
CENTAR GRADA	Town centre
GARAŽA	Garage
JEDAN SMER	One-way street
KAMP	Camping site
KRAJ ZABRANE	End of no-parking zone
MILICIJA	Militia (police)
OSIM ZA VOZILA...	Except for vehicles...
OPASNOST	Danger
ODRON KAMENA	Falling rocks
OPASNO KAD PADA KIŠA	Dangerous when wet
OGRANIČENA BRZINA ZBOG DOTRAJALOG KOLOVOZA	Limited speed — bad road surface
OPASNA KRIVINA	Dangerous bend (curve)
PAZI NA VOZ [VLAK]	Caution — level (railroad crossing)
PALI SVETLA	Turn on lights
RADOVI NA PUTU	Road works (men working)
STOJ	Stop
ŠKOLA	School
VOZ [VLAK]	Train
VELIKI NAGIB	Steep hill
ZABRANJENO PARKIRANJE	No parking
ZABRANJENO PRETICANJE	No overtaking (passing)
ZABRANJEN ULAZ	No entry
ZABRANJENO SKRETANJE	No turning (right or left)

Motorway telephone

On the main *autoput* (**ah**ootopoot–motorway or freeway),
there are telephone posts for emergency, breakdowns and
accidents at five-kilometre intervals. Call 987, *Auto-Moto
Savez Jugoslavije* (AMSJ), the Car Drivers' Association of
Yugoslavia.

FOR INTERNATIONAL ROAD SIGNS, see pages 160-161

FOR INTERNATIONAL ROAD SIGNS, see pages 160-161

CAR – INFORMATION

Part B

Accidents

This section is confined to immediate aid. The legal problems of responsibility and settlement can be taken care of at a later stage.

Your first concern will be for the injured.

Is anyone hurt?	Da li je neko povredjen?	dah lee yeh nehko povrehjehn
Don't move.	Nemojte se pokretati.	nehmoyteh seh pokrehtahtee
It's all right. Don't worry.	Sve je u redu. Ne brinite se.	sveh yeh oo rehdoo. neh breeneeteh seh
Where's the nearest telephone?	Gde je najbliži telefon?	gdeh yeh nahybleezhee tehlehfon
Can I use your phone? There's been an accident.	Mogu li se poslužiti Vašim telefonom. Desio se nesrećan slučaj.	mogoo lee seh posloozheeteh vahsheem tehlehfonom. dehseeo seh nehsrehchahn sloochahy
Call a doctor (ambulance) quickly.	Pozovite doktora (kola za hitnu pomoć), brzo.	pozoveeteh doktorah (kolah zah heetnoo pomoch) berzo
There are people injured.	Ima povredjenih.	eemah povrehjehneeh
Help me get them out of the car.	Pomozite mi da ih izvadimo iz kola.	pomozeeteh mee dah eeh eezvahdeemo eez kolah

Police – Exchange of information

Please call the police.	Pozovite, molim Vas policiju [miliciju].	pozoveeteh moleem vahs poleetseeyoo [meeleetseeyoo]
There's been an accident at... It's about 2 kilometres from...	Dogodio se nesrećni slučaj kod... Desio se otprilike 2 kilometra od...	dogodeeo seh nehsrehchnee sloochahy kod...dehseeo seh otpreeleekeh 2 keelomehtrah od
I'm on the Zagreb-Belgrade road, kilometer marker 50.	Ja sam na putu Zagreb-Beograd, kod 50 kilometra.	yah sahm nah pootoo zahgrehb behograhd kod 50 keelomehtrah

CAR – ACCIDENTS

Here's my name and address.	Izvolite moje ime i adresu.	eezvoleeteh moyeh eemeh ee ahdrehsoo
Would you mind acting as a witness?	Da li biste hteli da budete svedok?	dah lee beesteh htehlee dah boodehteh svehdok
I'd like an interpreter.	Želim tumača.	zhehleem toomahchah
Where's the nearest garage?	Gde je najbliža garaža?	gdeh yeh nahybleezhah gahrahzhah

Remember to put out a red triangle warning if the car is out of action or impeding traffic.

Breakdown

...and that's what we'll do with this section: break it down into four phases.

1. **On the road:** You ask where the nearest garage is.
2. **At the garage:** You tell the mechanic what's wrong.
3. **Finding the trouble:** He tells you what he thinks is wrong.
4. **Getting it fixed:** You tell him to fix it and, once that's over, settle the account (or argue about it).

Phase 1 – On the road

Excuse me. My car has broken down. May I use your phone?	Izvinite. Kola su mi se pokvarila. Mogu li se poslužiti Vašim telefonom?	eezveeneeteh. kolah soo mee seh pokvahreelah. mogoo lee seh posloozheetee vahsheem tehlehfonom
What's the telephone number of the nearest garage?	Koji je broj najbliže garaže?	koyee yeh broy nahybleezheh gahrahzheh
I've had a breakdown at...	Kola su mi u kvaru kod...	kolah soo mee oo kvahroo kod

We are on the Ljubljana-Zagreb motorway, about 10 kilometres from Zagreb.	Mi smo na autoputu Ljubljana-Zagreb, oko 10 kilometara od Zagreba.	mee smo nah **ah**ootopootoo lʸoobl'ahnah zahgrehb oko 10 **kee**lomehtahrah od **zah**grehbah
Can you send a mechanic?	Možete li poslati mehaničara?	**mo**zhehteh lee **po**slahtee mehh**hah**neechahrah
Can you send a truck to tow my car?	Možete li poslati kamion da šlepuje moja kola?	**mo**zhehteh lee po**slah**tee kah**mee**on dah **shleh**pooyeh **mo**yah kolah
How long will you be?	Kad možete biti ovde?	kahd **mo**zhehteh **bee**tee **ov**deh

Phase 2 – At the garage

Can you help me?	Možete li mi pomoći?	**mo**zhehteh lee mee **po**mochee
Are you the mechanic?	Da li ste Vi mehaničar?	dah lee steh vee mehh**hah**neechahr
I don't know what's wrong with it.	Ja ne znam šta nije u redu.	yah neh znahm shtah **nee**yeh oo **reh**doo
I think there's something wrong with the...	Ja mislim da nešto nije u redu sa...	yah **mee**sleem dah **neh**shto **nee**yeh oo **reh**doo sah
battery	akumulatorom	ahkoo**moo**lahtorom
brakes	kočnicama	**koch**neetsahmah
bulbs	sijalicama	**see**yahleetsahmah
clutch	kuplungom	**koo**ploongom
cooling system	sistemom za hladjenje	**see**stehmom zah **hlah**jehñeh
contact	kontaktima	kon**tahk**teemah
dimmers	oborenim svetlom	oborehneem **sveh**tlom
dynamo	dinamom	dee**nah**mom
electrical system	električnim sistemom	ehl**ehk**treechneem **see**stehmom
engine	motorom	**mo**torom
gears	menjačem brzina	meh**nah**chehm ber**zee**nah
handbrake	ručnom kočnicom	**rooch**nom **koch**neetsom
headlight	prednjim farovima	**prehd**ñeem **fah**roveemah
horn	sirenom	**see**rehnom
ignition system	sistemom paljenja	**see**stehmom **pahl'**ehnah
indicator	žmigavcima	**zhmee**gahvtseemah

CAR – REPAIRS

lights	svetlima	svehtleemah
brake light	svetlom za kočnice	svehtlom zah kochneetseh
reversing (back up) light	svetlom za vožnju u nazad	svehtlom zah vozhñoo oo nahzahd
tail lights	stražnjim svetlima	strahzhñeem svehtleemah
lubrication system	sistemom podmazivanja	seestehmom podmazeevahñah
pedal	pedalom	pehdahlom
reflectors	reflektorima	rehflehktoreemah
sparking plugs	kablom za svećice	kahblom zah svehcheetseh
starting motor	startnim motorom	stahrtneem motorom
steering	upravljanjem	ooprahvl‚ahñehm
suspension	amortizerima	ahmorteezehreemah
transmission	transmisijom	trahns meeseeyom
wheels	točkovima	tochkoveemah
wipers	brisačima	breesahcheemah

RIGHT	LEFT	FRONT	BACK
DESNO	**LEVO**	**SPREDA**	**POZADI**
(**deh**sno)	(**leh**vo)	(**spreh**dah)	(po**zah**dee)

It's...	To je...	to yeh
bad	loše	losheh
blowing	ne zatvara	neh zahtvarah
blown	pregorelo	prehgorehlo
broken	razbijeno	rahzbeeyehno
burnt	pregoreno	prehgorehno
cracked	napuknuto	nahpooknooto
defective	defektno	dehfehktno
disconnected	prekinuto	prehkeenooto
dry	suvo	soovo
frozen	smrznuto	smerznooto
jammed	zaglavljeno	zahglahvl‚ehno
knocking	lupa	loopah
leaking	curi	tsooree
loose	labavo	lahbahvo
misfiring	pogrešno pali	pogrehshno pahlee
noisy	bučno	boochno
not working	ne radi	neh rahdee
overheating	pregrejavanje	prehgreeyahvahneh

short-circuiting	kratki spoj	krahtkee spoy
slack	popustilo	popoosteelo
slipping	spada	spahdah
stuck	zaglavljeno	zahglahvl^yehno
vibrating	vibrira	veebreerah
weak	slabo	slahbo
worn	dotrajalo	dotrahyahlo

The car won't start.	Auto neće da se upali.	ahooto nehcheh dah seh oopahlee
It's locked and the keys are inside.	Zaključano je a ključevi su unutra.	zahkl^yoochahno yeh ah kl^yoochehvee soo oonootrah
The fan-belt is too slack.	Kaiš ventilatora je popustio.	kaheesh vehnteelahtorah yeh popoosteeo
The radiator is leaking.	Radijator curi.	rahdeeyahtor tsooree
The idling needs adjusting.	Brzi (polagani) hod treba da se podesi.	berzee (polahgahnee) hod trehbah dah seh podehsee
The clutch engages too quickly.	Kuplung hvata suviše brzo.	kooploong hvahtah sooveesheh berzo
The steering wheel's vibrating.	Kolo volana vibrira.	kolo volahnah veebreerah
The wipers are smearing.	Brisači zapinju.	breesahchee zahpeeñoo
The pneumatic suspension is weak.	Pneumatski amortizer je slab.	pnehoomahtskee ahmorteezehr yeh slahb
The pedal needs adjusting.	Pedala treba da se podesi.	pehdahlah trehbah dah seh podehsee

Now that you've explained what's wrong, you'll want to know how long it'll take to repair it and arrange yourself accordingly:

How long will it take to repair?	Koliko će trajati popravak?	koleeko cheh trahyahtee poprahvahk
How long will it take to find out what's wrong?	Koliko će trajati da pronadjate šta nije u redu?	koleeko cheh trahyahtee dah pronahjehteh shtah neeyeh oo rehdoo
Suppose I come back in half an hour (tomorrow)?	Mogu li da dodjem za pola sata (sutra)?	mogoo lee dah dojehm zah polah sahtah (sootrah)

Can you give me a lift into town?	**Možete li me povesti do grada?**	mozhehteh lee meh povehstee do grahdah
Is there a place to stay nearby?	**Da li mogu odsesti negde u blizini?**	dah lee mogoo odsehstee nehgdeh oo bleezeenee
May I use your phone?	**Mogu li upotrebiti Vaš telefon?**	mogoo lee oopotrehbeetee vahsh tehlehfon

Phase 3 – Finding the trouble

It's up to the mechanic either to find the trouble or to repair it. All you have to do is hand him the book and point to the text in Serbo-Croatian below.

Molim Vas pogledajte ovu abecednu listu i pokažite deo koji je u kvaru. Ako Vaša mušterija želi da zna šta nije u redu sa tim delom, nadjite odgovarajući naziv na sledećoj listi (polomljen, kratki spoj itd).*

CAR – REPAIRS

akumulator	battery
amortizer	shock absorber
amortizer	suspension
automatski prenos	automatic transmission
bobina	ignition coil
brzina	gear
cilinder	cylinder
ćelije akumulatora	battery cells
četke	brushes
dijafragma	diaphragm
dinamo	dynamo
dugmad	points
električni sistem	electrical system
filter	filter
filter benzina	petrol filter
filter za ulje	oil filter
filter za vazduh	air filter
generator	generator
glava cilindera	cylinder head

* Please look at the following alphabetical list and point to the defective item. If your customer wants to know what's wrong with it, pick the applicable item from the next list (broken, short-circuited, etc.).

glavni ležaj	main bearings
glava motora	block
kabl	cable
karburator	carburettor
kardanski zglob	universal joint
klip	piston
kočnica	brake
kočni cilinder	brake drum
kontakt	contact
kuplung	clutch
kurbla	crankcase
kutija upravljača	steering box
kutija menjača	gear box
ležaj	bearing
ležišta u sponi	track rod ends
masnoća	grease
motor	engine
motor startera	starter motor
obloga kočnice	lining
opruga ventila	valve spring
opruge	springs
osovina	shaft
papučice	shoes
pedala kuplunga	clutchpedal
ploča kuplunga	clutch plate
plovak	float
pneumatski amortizer	pneumatic suspension
poluga prebacivača	dipswitch
potisne opruge	pressure springs
prenos	transmission
prstenovi	rings
prstenovi klipa	piston rings
pumpa	pump
pumpa benzina	fuel pump
pumpa za vodu	water pump
pumpa uštrcavanja	injection pump
radijator	radiator
radilica	crankshaft
razvodnik	distributor
remen ventilatora	fan-belt
rotor elektro pokretača	starter armature
sistem hladjenja	cooling system
spojnice	joint
stabilizator	stabilizer
stub upravljača	steering column
svećice	sparking plugs

CAR – REPAIRS

tekućina akumulatora	battery liquid
termostat	thermostat
točkovi	wheels
upravljač	steering
ventil	valve
ventilator	fan
ventili	stems
veza	connection
vodovi razvodnika	distributor leads
vodovi svećica	sparking-plug leads
zaptivač glave cilindera	cylinder head gasket
zazori	tappets
zupčanici	teeth
zupčanik	camshaft
zupčasta poluga i zupčanik	rack and pinion

Sledeća lista sadrži reči za opis kvara kao i ono što treba da se popravi na kolima.*

brzo	quick
curi	leaking
čistiti	to clean
defektan	defective
demontirati	to strip down
dotrajalo	worn
isisavati	to bleed
iskrivljen	warped
izbalansirati	to balance
izgoreno	burnt
izmeniti	to change
kratak	short
kratak spoj	short-circuit
labavo	loose
lupa	knocking
napuknuto	cracked
napuniti	to charge
ne zatvara	blowing
nisko	low

* The following list contains words about what's wrong as well as what may need to be done with the car.

pogrešno paljenje	misfiring
popustilo	slack
popustiti	to loosen
pregorelo	blown
pregrejavanje	overheating
prekinut	disconnected
prljav	dirty
probušeno	puncture
radi	play
razbijeno	broken
slabo	weak
smrznut	frozen
spada	slipping
stegnuti	to tighten
suvo	dry
šlajfovati	to grind in
štelovanje	to adjust
vibrira	vibrating
visok	high
zaglavito	stuck
zaglavljeno	jammed
zameniti	to reline
zameniti	to replace
zardjalo	corroded

Phase 4 – Getting it fixed

Have you found the trouble?	**Da li ste pronašli kvar?**	dah lee steh **pro**nahshlee kvahr

Now that you know what's wrong, or at least have some idea, you'll want to find out…

Is that serious?	**Da li je to ozbiljno?**	dah lee yeh to **oz**beelʸno
Can you fix it?	**Možete li to popraviti?**	**mo**zhehteh lee to po**prah**veetee
Can you do it now?	**Možete li to uraditi sada?**	**mo**zhehteh lee to oo**rah**deetee **sah**dah
What's it going to cost?	**Koliko će koštati?**	**ko**leeko cheh **ko**shtahtee

| Have you the necessary spare parts? | **Imate li potrebne rezervne delove?** | eemahteh lee **potrehbneh rehzehrvneh dehloveh** |

What if he says "no"?

Why can't you do it?	**Zašto to ne možete uraditi?**	**zash**to to neh **mozhehteh** **oorah**deetee
Is it essential to have that part?	**Da li je taj deo neophodan?**	dah lee yeh tahy **deho nehophodahn**
How long is it going to take to get the spare parts?	**Koliko će trebati da dobijete te rezervne delove?**	koleeko cheh **trehbahtee** dah **dobeeyehteh** teh **rehzehrvneh dehloveh**
Where's the nearest garage that can repair it?	**Gde je najbliža garaža gde se to može popraviti?**	gdeh yeh **nahybleezhah** gahrah**zhah** gdeh seh to **mozheh** poprah**veetee**
Well, can you fix it so that I can get as far as…?	**Možete li to popraviti tako da stignem do…?**	**mozhehteh** lee to poprah**veetee** tahko dah **steeg**nehm do

If you're really stuck, ask if you can leave the car at the garage. Contact an automobile association or hire another car.

Settling the bill?

| Is everything fixed? | **Da li je sve u redu?** | dah lee yeh sveh oo **reh**doo |
| How much do I owe you? | **Koliko Vam dugujem?** | koleeko vahm **doogooyehm** |

The garage then presents you with a bill. If you're satisfied…

| Will you take a traveller's cheque (check)? | **Da li primate putni ček?** | dah lee **pree**mahteh **poot**nee chehk |
| Thanks very much for your help. | **Hvala Vam mnogo za Vašu pomoć.** | **hvah**lah vahm **mno**go zah **vah**shoo **pomo**ch |

This is for you.	**Ovo je za Vas.**	ovo yeh zah vahs

But you may think that the workmanship is sloppy or that you're paying for work not done. Get the bill itemized. If necessary, get it translated before you pay.

I'd like to check the bill first. Would you itemize the work done?	**Želim da prekontrolišem račun prvo. Naznačite, molim Vas, šta je sve uradjeno.**	zehleem dah prehkontroleeshehm rahchoon pervo. nahznahcheeteh moleem vahs shtah yeh sveh oorahjehno

If the garage won't back down – and you're still sure you're right – get the help of a third party.

Some international road signs

No vehicles

No entry

No overtaking (passing)

Oncoming traffic has priority

Maximum speed limit

No parking

Caution

Intersection

Dangerous bend (curve)

Road narrows

Intersection with secondary road

Two-way traffic

Dangerous hill

Uneven road

Falling rocks

Give way (yield)

Main road, thoroughfare

End of restriction

One-way traffic

Traffic goes this way

Roundabout (rotary)

Bicycles only

Pedestrians only

Minimum speed limit

Keep right (left if symbol reversed)

Parking

Hospital

Motorway (expressway)

Motor vehicles only

Filling station

No through road

Doctor

Frankly, how much use is a phrase book going to be to you in case of serious injury or illness? The only phrase you need in such an emergency is…

Get a doctor – quick!	**Zovite doktora, brzo!**	zoveeteh **dok**torah **ber**zo

But there are minor aches and pains, ailments and irritations that can upset the best planned trip. Here we can help you – and, perhaps, the doctor.

Some doctors will speak English well; others will know enough for your needs. But suppose there is something the doctor cannot explain because of language difficulties? We've thought of that. As you will see, this section has been arranged to enable you and the doctor to communicate. From page 165 to 171, you find your side of the dialogue on the upper half of each page; the doctor's is on the lower half.

The whole section has been divided into three parts: illness, wounds, nervous tension. Page 171 is concerned with prescriptions and fees.

General

I need a doctor – quickly.	**Treba mi doktor, brzo.**	**treh**bah mee **dok**tor **ber**zo
Can you get me a doctor?	**Možete li mi naći doktora?**	**mo**zhehteh lee mee **nah**chee **dok**torah
Is there a doctor in the hotel?	**Da li u hotelu ima doktor?**	dah lee oo ho**teh**loo **ee**mah **dok**tor
Please telephone for a doctor immediately.	**Molim Vas pozovite doktora odmah.**	**mo**leem vahs pozo**vee**teh **dok**torah **od**mah
Where's there a doctor who speaks English?	**Gde ima doktor koji govori engleski?**	gdeh **ee**mah **dok**tor **ko**yee **go**voree **ehn**glehskee
Is there an American/ English hospital in the town?	**Ima li u gradu američka/engleska bolnica?**	**ee**mah lee oo **grah**doo ah**meh**reechkah/**ehn**glehskah **bol**neetsah

FOR CHEMIST, see page 108

Where's the doctor's office (surgery)?	**Gde je ordinacija lekara?**	gdeh yeh ordee**nahts**eeyah lehkahrah
What are the office (surgery) hours?	**Kad lekar ordinira?**	kahd lehkahr ordeeneerah
Could the doctor come and see me here?	**Da li bi doktor mogao da dodje ovde da me pregleda?**	dah lee bee doktor mogaho dah dojeh ovdeh dah meh prehglehdah
What time can the doctor come?	**Kad može doktor da dodje?**	kahd mozheh doktor dah dojeh

Note: Doctors in Yugoslavia don't have private consulting rooms, except for a few in Zagreb and Ljubljana.

Symptoms

Use this section to tell the doctor what's wrong. Basically, what he'll require to know is:

What? (ache, pain, bruise, etc.)
Where? (arm, stomach, etc.)
How long? (have you had the trouble)

Before you visit the doctor, find out the answers to these questions by glancing through the pages that follow. In this way, you'll save valuable time.

Parts of the body

ankle	**članak**	chlahnahk
appendix	**slepo crevo**	slehpo tsrehvo
arm	**ruka**	rookah
artery	**arterija**	ahrtehreeyah
back	**ledja**	lehjah
bladder	**mehur**	mehhoor
blood	**krv**	kerv
bone	**kost**	kost
bowels	**creva**	tsrehvah
breast	**grudi**	groodee
cheek	**obraz**	obrahz
chest	**grudi**	groodee
chin	**brada**	brahdah
collar-bone	**ključna kost**	kl'oochnah kost
ear	**uvo**	oovo
elbow	**lakat**	lahkaht

eye	oko	oko
eyes	oči	ochee
face	lice	leetseh
finger	prst	perst
foot	stopalo	stopahlo
forehead	čelo	chehlo
gland	žlezda	zhlehzdah
hand	šaka	shahkah
head	glava	glahvah
heart	srce	sertseh
heel	peta	pehtah
hip	kuk	kook
intestines	creva	tsrehvah
jaw	vilica	veeleetsah
joint	zglavak	zglahvahk
kidney	bubreg	boobrehg
knee	koleno	kolehno
knee cap	čašica kolena	chahsheetsah kolehnah
leg	noga	nogah
lip	usna	oosnah
liver	jetra	yehtrah
lungs	pluća	ploochah
mouth	usta	oostah
muscle	mišić	meesheech
neck	vrat	vraht
nerve	živac	zheevahts
nose	nos	nos
rib	rebro	rehbro
shoulder	rame	rahmeh
skin	koža	kozhah
spine	kičma	keechmah
stomach	stomak	stomahk
tendon	žila	zheelah
thigh	bedro	behdro
throat	grlo	gerlo
thumb	palac	pahlahts
toe	prst na nozi	perst nah nozee
tongue	jezik	yehzeek
tonsils	krajnici	krahyneetsee
urine	urin	ooreen
vein	vena	vehnah
wrist	ručni zglavak	roochnee zglahvahk

LEFT/ON THE LEFT SIDE **LEVO/NA LEVOJ STRANI** (lehvo/nah léhvoy strahnee)	RIGHT/ON THE RIGHT SIDE **DESNO/NA DESNOJ STRANI** (dehsno/nah dehsnoy strahnee)

PATIENT

Part 1 – Illness

I'm not feeling well.	**Ja se ne osećam dobro.**	yah seh neh osehchahm dobro
I'm ill.	**Bolestan sam.**	bolehstahn sahm
I've got a pain here.	**Ovde me boli.**	ovdeh meh bolee
His/Her... hurts.	**Njegov/Njegova... boli.**	ñehgov/ñehgovah... bolee
I've got a...	**Ja imam...**	yah eemahm
headache	**glavobolju**	glahvobol'oo
backache	**bolove u ledjima**	boloveh oo lehjeemah
fever	**groznicu**	grozneetsah
sore throat	**gušobolju**	gooshobol'oo
I'm constipated.	**Imam zatvor.**	eemahm zahtvor
I've been vomiting.	**Povraća mi se.**	povrahchah mee seh

DOCTOR

Bolest

Na šta se žalite?	What's the trouble?
Gde Vas boli?	Where does it hurt?
Koliko dugo Vas to boli?	How long have you had this pain?
Kako dugo se ovako osećate?	How long have you been feeling like this?
Zavrnite rukav.	Roll up your sleeve.
Molim Vas skinite se (do pojasa).	Please undress (down to the waist).
Molim Vas skinite pantalone i gaćice.	Please remove your trousers and underpants.

DOCTOR

PATIENT

I feel ill/faint.	**Ja se osećam bolestan/slab.**	yah seh osehchahm bolehstahn/slahb
I feel sick/I'm dizzy.	**Zlo mi je/Vrti mi se u glavi.**	zlo mee yeh/**vertee** mee seh oo **glah**vee
I feel nauseated/I feel shivery.	**Muka mi je/ Grozničav sam.**	**mookah** mee yeh/ grozn**ee**chahv sahm
I/He/She's got a/an...	**Ja/on/ona ima...**	yah/on/onah **ee**mah
abcess	**abces**	**ahb**tsehs
asthma	**astmu**	**ahst**moo
boil	**čir**	cheer
chill	**prehladu**	**prehh**lahdoo
cold	**prehladu**	**prehh**lahdoo
constipation	**zatvor**	**zah**tvor
convulsions	**grčeve**	**ger**chehveh
cramps	**grčeve**	**ger**chehveh
diarrhoea	**proliv**	**pro**leev
fever	**groznicu**	**groz**neetsoo
haemorrhoids	**hemoroide**	hehmoro**ee**deh
hay fever	**sensku groznicu**	**sehn**skoo **groz**neetsoo

DOCTOR

Molim Vas lezite ovde.	Please lie down over here.
Otvorite usta.	Open your mouth.
Duboko dišite.	Breathe deeply.
Kašljite, molim Vas.	Cough, please.
Izmeriću Vam temperaturu.	I'll take your temperature.
Izmeriću Vam krvni pritisak.	I'm going to take your blood pressure.
Da li je ovo prvi put da ste to dobili?	Is this the first time you've had this?

PATIENT

hernia	hernija	hehrneeyah
indigestion	nevarenje	nehvahrehñeh
inflammation of...	upala...	oopahlah
influenza	grip	greep
morning sickness	jutarnja mučnina	yootahrñah moochneenah
stiff neck	ukočen vrat	ookochehn vraht
rheumatism	reumatizam	rehoomahteezahm
sunburn	opekotine od sunca	opehkoteeneh od soontsah
sunstroke	sunčanica	soonchahneetsah
tonsillitis	upala krajnika	oopahlah krahyneekah
ulcer	čir	cheer
whooping cough	veliki kašalj	vehleekee kahshahlʸ

| It's nothing serious, I hope? | Nadam se da nije ništa ozbiljno? | nahdahm seh dah neeyeh neeshtah ozbeelʸno |
| I'd like you to pre-scribe me some medicine. | Želeo bih da mi prepišete neki lek. | zhehleho beeh dah mee prehpeeshehteh nehkee lehk |

DOCTOR

Nije ništa zabrinjavajuće.	It's nothing to worry about.
Morate ostati u krevetu... dana.	You must stay in bed for...days.
Vi imate...	You've got...
prehladu/artritis/upalu pluća grip/trovanje hranom upalu...	a cold/arthritis/pneumonia influenza/food poisoning an inflammation of...
Vi pušite/pijete previše.	You're smoking/drinking too much.
Vi ste premoreni. Potreban vam je mir.	You're over-tired. You need a rest.
Treba da idete kod specijaliste.	I want you to see a specialist.
Treba da idete u bolnicu na jedan kompletni pregled.	I want you to go to the hospital for a general check-up.
Prepisaću vam antibiotike.	I'll prescribe an antibiotic.

DOCTOR

PATIENT

I'm a diabetic.	**Ja sam dijabetičar.**	yah sahm deeyah**beh**teechahr
I have a cardiac condition.	**Bolujem od srca.**	bolooyehm od **ser**tsah
I had a heart attack in...	**Imao sam srčani napad u...**	**ee**maho sahm **ser**chahnee nahpahd oo
I'm allergic to...	**Ja sam alergičan na...**	yah sahm ah**lehr**geechahn nah
This is my usual medicine.	**Ovo je moj uobičajeni lek.**	ovo yeh moy oooo**bee**chahyehnee lehk
I need this medicine.	**Ja trebam ovaj lek.**	yah **treh**bahm ovahy lehk
I'm expecting a baby.	**Ja očekujem bebu.**	yah ochehkooyehm **beh**boo
Can I travel?	**Mogu li putovati?**	mogoo lee **poo**tovahtee

DOCTOR

DOCTOR

Koliku dozu insulina uzimate?	What dose of insulin are you taking?
Inekciju ili oralno?	Injection or oral?
Kako ste se lečili?	What treatment have you been having?
Koji ste lek uzimali?	What medicine have you been taking?
Vi ste imali (mali) srčani napad.	You've had a (slight) heart attack.
Mi ne upotrebljavamo...u Jugoslaviji. Ovo je vrlo slično.	We don't use...in Yugoslavia. This is very similar.
Kad očekujete bebu?	When is the baby due?
Vi ne možete putovati do...	You can't travel until...

PATIENT

Part 2 – Wounds

Could you have a look at this...?	**Možete li pogledati...?**	mozhehteh lee pogledahtee
blister	**plik**	pleek
boil	**potkožni čir**	potkozhnee cheer
bruise	**modricu**	modreetsoo
burn	**opekotinu**	opehkoteenoo
cut	**posekotinu**	posehkoteenoo
graze	**ogrebotinu**	ogrehboteenoo
insect bite	**ubod insekta**	oobod eensehktah
lump	**čvorugu**	chvoroogoo
rash	**osip**	oseep
sting	**ubod**	oobod
swelling	**otok**	otok
wound	**ranu**	rahnoo
I can't move my...	**Ja ne mogu da**	yah neh mogoo dah
It hurts.	**pomaknem...**	pomahknehm...
	Boli me.	bolee meh

DOCTOR

Ozlede

To je (nije) inficirano.	It's (not) infected.
Imate diskus.	You've got a slipped disc.
Treba da odete na rentgen.	I want you to have an X-ray.
To je...	It's...
prelomljeno/istegnuto iščašeno/razderano	broken/sprained dislocated/torn
Istegli ste mišić.	You've pulled a muscle.
Daću Vam antiseptik. Nije ništa ozbiljno.	I'll give you an antiseptic. It's not serious.
Dodjite ponovo za...dana.	I want you to come and see me in...days time.

DOCTOR

PATIENT

Part 3 – Nervous tension

I'm in a nervous state.	**Nervozan sam.**	**nehr**vozahn sahm
I'm feeling depressed.	**Osećam se deprimi-rano.**	osehchahm seh deh**pree**mee-rahno
I want some sleeping pills.	**Želeo bih tablete za spavanje.**	**zheh**leho beeh tah**bleh**teh zah spahvahñeh
I can't eat/I can't sleep.	**Ne mogu da jedem/ Ne mogu da spavam.**	neh mogoo dah **yeh**dehm/ neh mogoo dah **spah**vahm
I'm having nightmares.	**Imam grozne snove.**	**ee**mahm groz**neh** snoveh
Can you prescribe a...?	**Možete li mi prepisati...?**	**mo**zhehteh lee mee preh**pee**sahteh
sedative/ tranquillizer	**sredstvo za umirenje**	**srehd**stvo zah oomeereh**ñeh**
anti-depressant	**sredstvo protiv depresije**	**srehd**stvo proteev deh**preh**seeyeh

---

DOCTOR

Nervna napetost

Vi patite od nervne napetosti.	You're suffering from nervous tension.
Vama je potreban mir.	You need a rest.
Koje tablete ste uzimali?	What pills have you been taking?
Koliko na dan?	How many a day?
Koliko dugo se ovako osećate?	How long have you been feeling like this?
Prepisaću Vam neke tablete.	I'll prescribe some tablets.
Daću Vam sredstvo za umirenje.	I'll give you a sedative.

PATIENT

Prescriptions and dosage

What kind of medicine is this?	**Kakav je ovo lek?**	kahkahv yeh ovo lehk
How many times a day should I take it?	**Koliko puta dnevno ga moram uzimati?**	koleeko pootah dnehvno gah morahm oozeemahtee
Must I swallow them whole?	**Moram li ih cele progutati?**	morahm lee eeh tsehleh progootahtee

Fee

How much do I owe you?	**Koliko sam Vam dužan?**	koleeko sahm vahm doozhahn
Do I pay you now or will you send me your bill?	**Da li da Vam odmah platim ili ćete mi poslati račun?**	dah lee dah vahm odmah plahteem eelee chehteh mee poslahtee rahchoon
Thanks for your help, doctor.	**Hvala Vam na pomoći, doktore.**	hvahlah vahm nah pomochee doktoreh

---

DOCTOR

Recepti i doziranja

Uzmite od ove medicine... malu kašiku svaka... sata.	Take... teaspoonful of this this medicine every... hours.
Uzmite... tablete sa čašom vode.	Take... pills with a glass of water.
... puta dnevno	... times a day
pre svakog obroka	before each meal
posle svakog obroka	after each meal
u jutro	in the morning
u veče	at night

Naplata honorara

To je..., molim Vas.	That's..., please.
Molim Vas platite mi sada.	Please pay me now.
Poslaću Vam račun.	I'll send you a bill.

FOR NUMBERS, see page 175

Dentist

Can you recommend a good dentist?	**Možete li mi pre- poručiti dobrog zubnog lekara?**	mozhehteh lee mee prehpo- roocheetee dobrog zoobnog lehkahrah
Can I make an (urgent) appointment to see the doctor...?	**Mogu li da zakažem (hitan) sastanak sa doktorom...?**	mogoo lee dah zahkahzhehm (heetahn) sahstahnahk sah doktorom
Can't you possibly make it earlier than that?	**Da li ikako može ranije?**	dah lee eekahko mozheh rahneeyeh
I've a toothache.	**Ja imam zubobolju.**	yah eemahm zoobobol'roo
I've an abcess.	**Ja imam abces.**	yah eemahm ahbtsehs
This tooth hurts.	**Ovaj zub me boli.**	ovahy zoob meh bolee
at the top	**gore**	goreh
at the bottom	**dole**	doleh
in the front	**napred**	nahprehd
at the back	**pozadi**	pozahdee
Can you fix it temporarily?	**Možete li ga priv- remeno popraviti?**	mozhehteh lee gah preevrehmehno poprahveetee
I don't want it extracted (pulled).	**Ne želim da ga izvadim.**	neh zhehleem dah gah eezvahdeem
I've lost a filling.	**Ispala mi je plomba.**	eespahlah mee yeh plombah
The gum is very sore/ The gum is bleeding.	**Desni me jako bole/ Desni mi krvare.**	dehsnee meh yahko boleh/ dehsnee mee kervahreh

Dentures

I have broken this denture.	**Slomio (slomila*) sam protezu.**	slomeeo (slomeelah) sahm protehzoo
Can you repair this denture?	**Možete li popraviti ovu protezu?**	mozhehteh lee poprahveetee ovoo protehzoo
When will it be ready?	**Kad će biti gotovo?**	kahd cheh beetee gotovo

* Feminine. See Grammar.

Optician

I've broken my glasses.	**Razbio (razbila*) sam svoje naočale.**	rahzbeeo (rahzbeelah) sahm svoyeh nahochahleh
Can you repair them for me?	**Možete li ih popraviti?**	mozhehteh lee eeh poprahveetee
When will they be ready?	**Kad će biti gotove?**	kahd cheh beetee gotoveh
Can you change the lenses?	**Možete li promeniti stakla?**	mozhehteh lee promehneetee stahklah
I want some contact lenses.	**Želim kontaktna stakla.**	zhehleem kontahktnah stahklah
I want tinted lenses.	**Želim tamna stakla.**	zhehleem tahmnah stahklah
I'd like to buy a pair of binoculars.	**Želeo bih da kupim durbin.**	zhehleho beeh dah koopeem doorbeen
How much do I owe you?	**Koliko Vam dugujem?**	koleeko vahm doogooyehm
Do I pay you now or will you send me your bill?	**Treba li da Vam platim sada ili ćete mi poslati račun?**	trehbah lee dah vahm plahteem sahdah eelee chehteh mee poslahteh rahchoon

OPTICIAN

* Feminine. See Grammar.

FOR NUMBERS, see page 175

Reference section

Countries

This page will help you to explain where you're from, where you've been, and where you're going.

Africa	**Afrika**	ahfreekah
Albania	**Albanija**	ahlbahneeyah
Australia	**Australija**	ahoostrahleeyah
Austria	**Austrija**	ahoostreeyah
Belgium	**Belgija**	behlgeeyah
Bulgaria	**Bugarska**	boogahrskah
Canada	**Kanada**	kahnahdah
China	**Kina**	keenah
Czechoslovakia	**Čehoslovačka**	chehhoslovahchkah
Denmark	**Danska**	dahnskah
England	**Engleska**	ehnglehskah
Europe	**Evropa**	ehvropah
France	**Francuska**	frahntsooskah
Germany	**Nemačka**	nehmahchkah
Great Britain	**Velika Britanija**	vehleekah breetahneeyah
Greece	**Grčka**	gerchkah
Hungary	**Madjarska**	mahjahrskah
Ireland	**Irska**	eerskah
Italy	**Italija**	eetahleeyah
Netherlands	**Nizozemska**	neezozehmskah
New Zealand	**Novi Zeland**	novee zehlahnd
Norway	**Norveška**	norvehshkah
Poland	**Poljska**	polʸskah
Rumania	**Rumunija**	roomooneeyah
Scandinavia	**Skandinavija**	skahndeenahveeyah
Scotland	**Škotska**	shkotskah
South Africa	**Južna Afrika**	yoozhnah ahfreekah
Spain	**Španija**	shpahneeyah
Sweden	**Švedska**	shvehdskah
Switzerland	**Švajcarska**	shvahytsahrskah
Turkey	**Turska**	toorskah
USA	**Sjedinjene Američka Države**	syehdeeʸnehneh ahmehreechkeh derzhahveh
USSR	**Sovjetski Savez**	sovyehtskee sahvehz
Wales	**Vels**	vehls
Yugoslavia	**Jugoslavija**	yoogoslahveeyah

Numbers

0	nula	noolah
1	jedan	**yeh**dahn
2	dva	dvah
3	tri	tree
4	četiri	**cheh**teeree
5	pet	peht
6	šest	shehst
7	sedam	**seh**dahm
8	osam	osahm
9	devet	**deh**veht
10	deset	**deh**seht
11	jedanaest	yeh**dah**nahehst
12	dvanaest	**dvah**nahehst
13	trinaest	**tree**nahehst
14	četrnaest	cheh**ter**nahehst
15	petnaest	**peht**nahehst
16	šesnaest	**shehs**nahehst
17	sedamnaest	seh**dahm**nahehst
18	osamnaest	**osahm**nahehst
19	devetnaest	deh**veht**nahehst
20	dvadeset	**dvah**dehseht
21	dvadeset jedan	**dvah**dehseht **yeh**dahn
22	dvadeset dva	**dvah**dehseht dvah
23	dvadeset tri	**dvah**dehseht tree
24	dvadeset četiri	**dvah**dehseht **cheh**teeree
25	dvadeset pet	**dvah**dehseht peht
26	dvadeset šest	**dvah**dehseht shehst
27	dvadeset sedam	**dvah**dehseht **seh**dahm
28	dvadeset osam	**dvah**dehseht osahm
29	dvadeset devet	**dvah**dehseht **deh**veht
30	trideset	**tree**dehseht
31	trideset jedan	**tree**dehseht **yeh**dahn
32	trideset dva	**tree**dehseht dvah
33	trideset tri	**tree**dehseht tree
40	četrdeset	cheh**ter**dehseht
41	četrdeset jedan	cheh**ter**dehseht **yeh**dahn
42	četrdeset dva	cheh**ter**dehseht dvah
43	četrdeset tri	cheh**ter**dehseht tree
50	pedeset	peh**deh**seht
51	pedeset jedan	peh**deh**seht **yeh**dahn
52	pedeset dva	peh**deh**seht dvah
53	pedeset tri	peh**deh**seht tree
60	šezdeset	shehz**deh**seht
61	šezdeset jedan	shehz**deh**seht **yeh**dahn

62	**šezdeset dva**	shehz**deh**seht dvah
63	**šezdeset tri**	shehz**deh**seht tree
70	**sedamdeset**	sehdahm **deh**seht
71	**sedamdeset jedan**	sehdahm**deh**seht **yeh**dahn
72	**sedamdeset dva**	sehdahm**deh**seht dvah
73	**sedamdeset tri**	sehdahm**deh**seht tree
80	**osamdeset**	osahm**deh**seht
81	**osamdeset jedan**	osahm**deh**seht **yeh**dahn
82	**osamdeset dva**	osahm**deh**seht dvah
83	**osamdeset tri**	osahm**deh**seht tree
90	**devedeset**	dehveh**deh**seht
91	**devedeset jedan**	dehveh**deh**seht **yeh**dahn
92	**devedeset dva**	dehveh**deh**seht dvah
93	**devedeset tri**	dehveh**deh**seht tree
100	**sto**	sto
101	**sto jedan**	sto **yeh**dahn
102	**sto dva**	sto dvah
110	**sto deset**	sto **deh**seht
120	**sto dvadeset**	sto **dvah**dehseht
130	**sto trideset**	sto **tree**dehseht
140	**sto četrdeset**	sto **chehter**dehseht
150	**sto pedeset**	sto **peh**dehseht
160	**sto šezdeset**	sto **shehz**dehseht
170	**sto sedamdeset**	sto **sedahm**dehseht
180	**sto osamdeset**	sto **osahm**dehseht
190	**sto devedeset**	sto **dehveh**dehseht
200	**dve stotine**	dveh **sto**teeneh
300	**tri stotine**	tree **sto**teeneh
400	**četiri stotine**	chehteeree **sto**teeneh
500	**pet stotina**	peht **sto**teenah
600	**šest stotina**	shehst **sto**teenah
700	**sedam stotina**	**seh**dahm **sto**teenah
800	**osam stotina**	osahm **sto**teenah
900	**devet stotina**	**deh**veht **sto**teenah
1000	**jedna hiljada**	**yeh**dnah heel^yahdah
1100	**hiljadu sto**	heel^yahdoo sto
1200	**hiljadu i dvesta**	heel^yahdoo ee **dveh**stah
2000	**dve hiljade**	dveh heel^yahdeh
5000	**pet hiljada**	peht heel^yahdah
10,000	**deset hiljada**	**deh**seht heel^yahdah
50,000	**pedeset hiljada**	**peh**dehseht heel^yahdah
100,000	**sto hiljada**	sto heel^yahdah
1,000,000	**jedan milion**	**yeh**dahn meeleeon
1,000,000,000	**milijarda**	meeleeyahrdah

first	prvi	pervee
second	drugi	droogee
third	treći	trehchee
fourth	četvrti	chehtvertee
fifth	peti	pehtee
sixth	šesti	shehstee
seventh	sedmi	sehdmee
eighth	osmi	osmee
ninth	deveti	dehvehtee
tenth	deseti	dehsehtee
once	jedanput	yehdahnpoot
twice	dva puta	dvah pootah
three times	tri puta	tree pootah
a half	polovina	poloveenah
half a...	pola od...	polah od
half of...	pola...	polah
half (adj.)	pola	polah
a quarter	četvrt	chehtvert
one third	jedna trećina	yehdnah trehcheenah
a pair of...	par...	pahr
a dozen	tuce	tootseh
1985	hiljadu devet sto osamdeset pet	heel^yahdoo dehveht sto osahmdehseht peht
1987	hiljadu devet sto osamdeset sedam	heel^yahdoo dehveht sto osahmdehseht sehdahm
1990	hiljadu devet sto devedeset	heel^yahdoo dehveht sto dehvehdehseht

Time

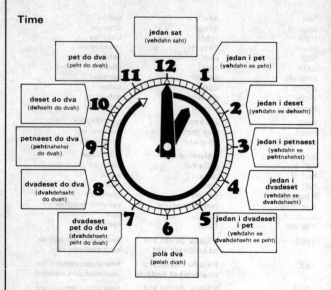

jedan sat (yehdahn saht)	
pet do dva (peht do dvah)	**jedan i pet** (yehdahn ee peht)
deset do dva (dehseht do dvah)	**jedan i deset** (yehdahn ee dehseht)
petnaest do dva (pehtnahehst do dvah)	**jedan i petnaest** (yehdahn ee pehtnahehst)
dvadeset do dva (dvahdehseht do dvah)	**jedan i dvadeset** (yehdahn ee dvahdehseht)
dvadeset pet do dva (dvahdehseht peht do dvah)	**jedan i dvadeset i pet** (yehdahn ee dvahdehseht ee peht)
pola dva (polah dvah)	

Useful expressions

What time is it?	**Koliko je sati?**	koleeko yeh sahtee
Excuse me. Can you tell me the time?	**Izvinite. Možete li mi reći koliko je sati?**	eezveeneeteh mozhehteh lee mee rehchee koleeko yeh sahtee
I'll meet you at... tomorrow.	**Sastaćemo se sutra u...**	sahstahchehmo seh sootrah oo
I am so sorry I'm late.	**Žao mi je što sam zakasnio.**	zhaho mee yeh shto sahm zahkahsneeo
after	**posle**	posleh
before	**pre**	preh
early	**rano**	rahno
in time	**na vreme**	nah vrehmeh
late	**kasno**	kahsno
midday (noon)	**podne**	podneh
midnight	**pola noći**	polah nochee

REFERENCE SECTION

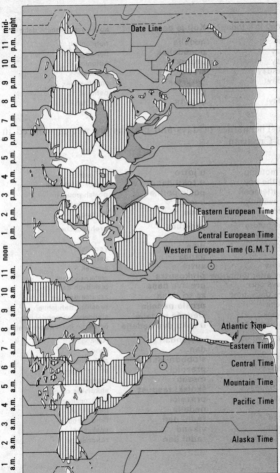

Countries which have adopted a time differing from that in the corresponding time zone. Note that in the USSR, official times is one hour ahead of the time in each corresponding time zone. In summer, numerous countries advance time one hour ahead of standard time.

REFERENCE SECTION

179

180

Days

What day is it today?	**Koji je danas dan?**	koyee yeh **dahnahs** dahn
Sunday	**nedelja**	nehdehlʲah
Monday	**ponedeljak**	ponehdehlʲahk
Tuesday	**utorak**	ootorahk
Wednesday	**sreda**	srehdah
Thursday	**četvrtak**	chehtvertahk
Friday	**petak**	pehtahk
Saturday	**subota**	soobotah

Note: The names of days and months are not capitalized in Serbo-Croatian.

in the morning	**u jutro**	oo yootro
during the day	**u toku dana**	oo tokoo dahnah
in the afternoon	**posle podne**	posleh podneh
in the evening	**u veče**	oovehcheh
at night	**noću**	nochoo
the day before yesterday	**prekjuče**	prehkyoocheh
yesterday	**juče**	yoocheh
today	**danas**	dahnahs
tomorrow	**sutra**	sootrah
the day after tomorrow	**prekosutra**	prehkosootrah
two days ago	**pre dva dana**	preh dvah dahnah
in three days' time	**za tri dana**	zah tree dahnah
last week	**prošle nedelje**	proshleh nehdehlʲeh
next week	**sledeće nedelje**	slehdehcheh nehdehlʲeh
during two weeks	**u toku dve nedelje**	oo tokoo dveh nehdehlʲeh
birthday	**rodjendan**	rojehndahn
day	**dan**	dahn
day off	**slobodni dan**	slobodnee dahn
holidays	**praznici**	prahzneetsee
month	**mesec**	mehsehts
school holidays	**školski raspust**	shkolskee raspoost
vacation	**praznici**	prahzneetsee
week	**nedelja**	nehdehlʲah
weekday	**radni dan**	rahdnee dahn
weekend	**vikend**	veekehnd
working day	**radni dan**	rahdnee dahn

Months

January	januar	yahnooahr
February	februar	fehbrooahr
March	mart	mahrt
April	april	ahpreel
May	maj	mahy
June	juni	yoonee
July	juli	yoolee
August	avgust	ahvgoost
September	septembar	sehptehmbahr
October	oktobar	oktobahr
November	novembar	novehmbahr
December	decembar	dehtsehmbahr
since June	od juna	od yoonah
during the month of August	za vreme meseca avgusta	zah vrehmeh mehsehtsah ahvgoostah
last month	prošlog meseca	proshlog mehsehtsah
next month	sledećeg meseca	slehdehchehg mehsehtsah
the month before	pre mesec dana	preh mehsehts dahnah
the next month	sledeći mesec	slehdehchee mehsehts
July 1st	prvog jula	pervog yoolah
March 17th	sedamnaestog	sehdahmnahehstog mahrtah

Letter headings are written thus:

Rijeka, August 17th, 19..   **Rijeka, 17. avgusta 19..**

Zagreb, July 1st, 19..   **Zagreb, 1. jula 19..**

Seasons

spring	proleće	prolehcheh
summer	leto	lehto
autumn	jesen	yehsehn
winter	zima	zeemah
in spring	u proleće	oo prolehcheh
during the summer	za vreme leta	zah vrehmeh lehtah
in autumn	u jesen	oo yehsehn
during the winter	za vreme zime	zah vrehmeh zeemeh

Public holidays

These are the main public holidays in Yugoslavia when banks,
offices and shops are closed:

New Year	**January 1st and 2nd**
Labour Days	**May 1st and 2nd**
Fighter's Day	**July 4th**
Days of the Republic	**November 29th and 30th**

These holidays are kept throughout the country. There is
another holiday, the Day of the Uprising of 1941, which differs
from region to region. Given below are the main regions and
the dates when they celebrate this holiday.

Bosnia and Herzegovina	**July 27th**
Croatia	**July 27th**
Istria and the Slovenian coast	**September 9th**
Macedonia	**October 11th and August 2nd**
Montenegro	**July 13th**
Serbia	**July 7th**
Slovenia	**July 22nd**

The year round...

Here are the average monthly temperatures in centigrade and
Fahrenheit for some Yugoslavian cities:

	Belgrade °C	°F	Ljubljana °C	°F	Dubrovnik °C	°F
January	0	31	−1	29	8	48
April	11	53	8	48	15	60
July	22	72	19	67	24	78
October	12	54	9	49	18	65

Conversion tables

To change centimetres into inches, multiply by .39.

To change inches into centimetres, multiply by 2.54.

Centimeters and inches

	in.	feet	yards
1 mm	0,039	0,003	0,001
1 cm	0,39	0,03	0,01
1 dm	3,94	0,32	0,10
1 m	39,40	3,28	1,09

	mm	cm	m
1 in.	25,4	2,54	0,025
1 ft.	304,8	30,48	0,304
1 yd.	914,4	91,44	0,914

(32 metres = 35 yards)

Temperature

To convert Centigrade into degrees Fahrenheit, multiply Centigrade by 1.8 and add 32.

To convert degrees Fahrenheit into Centigrade, subtract 32 from Fahrenheit and divide by 1.8.

REFERENCE SECTION

Metres and feet

The figure in the middle stands for both metres and feet, e.g., 1 metre = 3,281 ft. and 1 foot = 0,30 m.

Metres		Feet
0.30	1	3.281
0.61	2	6.563
0.91	3	9.843
1.22	4	13.124
1.52	5	16.403
1.83	6	19.686
2.13	7	22.967
2.44	8	26.248
2.74	9	29.529
3.05	10	32.810
3.35	11	36.091
3.66	12	39.372
3.96	13	42.635
4.27	14	45.934
4.57	15	49.215
4.88	16	52.496
5.18	17	55.777
5.49	18	59.058
5.79	19	62.339
6.10	20	65.620
7.62	25	82.023
15.24	50	164.046
22.86	75	246.069
30.48	100	328.092

Other conversion charts

For	see page
Clothing sizes	115
Currency converter	136
Customs allowances	23
Distance (miles-kilometres)	144
Fluid measures	142
Tire pressure	143

Weight conversion

The figure in the middle stands for both kilograms and pounds, e.g., 1 kilogram = 2.205 lb. and 1 pound = 0.45 kilograms.

Kilograms (kg.)		Avoirdupois pounds
0.45	1	2.205
0.90	2	4.405
1.35	3	6.614
1.80	4	8.818
2.25	5	11.023
2.70	6	13.227
3.15	7	15.432
3.60	8	17.636
4.05	9	19.840
4.50	10	22.045
6.75	15	33.068
9.00	20	44.889
11.25	25	55.113
22.50	50	110.225
33.75	75	165.338
45.00	100	220.450

REFERENCE SECTION

NORTH
SEVER
sehvehr

WEST
ZAPAD
zahpahd

EAST
ISTOK
eestok

SOUTH
JUG
yoog

Common abbreviations

Here are some common abbreviations you are likely to encounter.

br.	broj	number
DIN.	dinar	dinar
g.	gospodin	Mister
gdja.	gospodja	Mrs.
gdjica.	gospodjica	Miss
god.	godina	year
h-s	hrvatskosrpski	Croato-Serbian
itd.	i tako dalje	and so on
jedn.	jednina	singular
mn.	množina	plural
m.r.	muški rod	masculine
o.g.	ove godine	this year
o.m.	ovog meseca	this month
p.	para	para (coin)
raz.	razred	class-room
rkt.	rimokatolik	Roman Catholic
SFRJ	Socijalistička Federativna Republika Jugoslavija	Socialist Federal Republic of Yugoslavia
SR	Socijalistička Republika	Socialist Republic
s-h	srpskohrvatski	Serbo-Croatian
šk.god.	školska godina	school year
tel.	telefon	telephone
tj.	to jest	that is
ul.	ulica	street
ž.r.	ženski rod	feminine

What does that sign mean?

You are sure to encounter some of these signs or notices on your trip.

Dame	Ladies
Gospoda	Gentlemen
Guraj	Push
Hladno	Cold
Izlaz	Exit
Kasa	Cash desk, cashier's
Kucajte	Knock
Muškarci	Men
Nedeljom zatvoreno	Closed on Sundays
Ne diraj	Do not touch
Nepušači	Non-smokers
Obaveštenja	Information
Opasnost po život	Mortal danger
Otvoreno	Open
Pešaci	Pedestrians
Pušači	Smokers
Pušenje zabranjeno	No smoking
Radi od...do...	Open from...to...
Rasprodaja	Sale
Stoj	Stop
Toplo	Warm
Ulaz	Entrance
Ulaz slobodan	Entrance free
Ulaz zabranjen	No entrance
Visoki napon	High voltage
Vuci	Pull
Za izdavanje	To let
Zatvoreno	Closed
Zauzeto	Occupied
Zvonite	Ring

ČUVAJ SE PSA
BEWARE OF THE DOG

Emergency!

By the time the emergency is upon you it's too late to turn to
this page to find the Serbo-Croatian for "I'll scream if you…".
So have a look at this short list beforehand – and, if you want
to be on the safe side, learn the expressions shown in capitals.

Be quick	**Požurite**	pozhooreeteh
Call the police	**Zovite policiju**	zoveeteh poleetseeyoo
CAREFUL	**OPREZNO**	oprehzno
Come here	**Dodjite ovamo**	dojeeteh ovahmo
Come in	**Udjite**	oojeeteh
Danger	**Opasnost**	opahsnost
Fire	**Vatra**	vahtrah
Gas	**Gas [plin]**	gahs [pleen]
Get a doctor	**Zovite doktora**	zoveeteh doktorah
Go away	**Odlazite**	odlahzeeteh
HELP	**U POMOĆ**	oopomoch
Get help quickly	**Dovedite pomoć, brzo**	dovehdeeteh pomoch berzo
I'm ill	**Bolestan (bolesna*) sam**	bolehstahn (bolehsnah) sahm
I'm lost	**Zalutao (zalutala*) sam**	zahlootaho (zahlootahlah) sahm
I've lost my…	**Izgubio sam svoj…**	eezgoobeeo sahm svoy
Leave me alone	**Ostavite me na miru**	ostahveeteh meh nah meeroo
Lie down	**Lezite**	lehzeeteh
Listen	**Slušajte**	slooshahyteh
Listen to me	**Slušajte me**	slooshahyteh meh
Look	**Pogledajte**	poglehdahyteh
LOOK OUT	**PAZITE**	pahzeeteh
POLICE	**POLICIJA**	poleetseeyah
Quick	**Brzo**	berzo
STOP	**STANITE**	stahneeteh
Stop here	**Stanite ovde**	stahneeteh ovdeh
Stop that man	**Zaustavite onog čoveka**	zahoostahveeteh onog chovehkah
STOP THIEF	**DRŽITE LOPOVA**	derzheeteh lopovah
Stop or I'll scream	**Prestanite ili ću vikati**	prehstahneeteh eelee choo veekahtee

* Feminine. See Grammar.

FOR CAR ACCIDENTS, see page 149

Emergency numbers

Ambulance ....

Fire ....

Police ....

Fill in these as well

Embassy ....

Consulate ....

Taxi ....

Airport information ....

Travel agent ....

Hotel ....

Restaurant ....

Babysitter ....

....

....

....

....

....

....

....

....

....

Index

Abbreviations	186		Doctor	162
Alphabet	7		Drinks	56
Arrival	22		Dry cleaning	126
Authors	105			
			Eating out	38
Baggage	24		alcoholic drinks	56
Ballet	82		appetizers	44
Bank	134		cheese	51
Beach	87		dessert	53
Body	163		egg dishes	45
Breakfast	34		fish	46
Bus	73		fowl	49
			fruit	52
Cables	138		game	49
Camping	89		meat	47
equipment	106		ordering	41
Car	142		seasonings	49
accidents	149		snacks	63
breakdown	150		soft drinks	62
parts	151		soups	45
rental	26		vegetables	49
repairs	154		Emergency	188
Casino	85			
Church services	79		Filling stations	142
Cinema	80		Friends	92
Coach	73			
Colours	112		Games	84
Concerts	82		Grammar	17
Countries	174			
Countryside	89		Hairdressing	121
Customs	23, 145		Hotel	28
			breakfast	34
Dancing	84		checking in	29
Dating	95		checking out	37
Days	180		difficulties	35
Dentist	172		registration	32
Directions	25, 144		service	33